D0166619

WHEN YOUR TEEN IS
STRUGGLING

MARK GREGSTON

HARVEST HOUSE PUBLISHERS

EUGENE, OREGON

Cover by Koechel Peterson & Associates, Inc., Minneapolis, Minnesota

Cover photos © Photos.com

This book contains stories in which the author has changed people's names and some details of their situations to protect their privacy.

WHEN YOUR TEEN IS STRUGGLING
Copyright © 2007 by Mark Gregston
Published by Harvest House Publishers
Eugene, Oregon 97402
www.harvesthousepublishers.com

Library of Congress Cataloging-in-Publication Data
Gregston, Mark, 1955-
    When your teen is struggling / Mark Gregston.
          p. cm.
    ISBN-13: 978-0-7369-1822-0 (pbk.)
    ISBN-10: 0-7369-1822-1 (pbk.)
    1. Parenting—Religious aspects—Christianity. 2. Parent and teenager—Religious aspects—Christianity. 3. Teenagers—Religious life. I. Title.
BV4529.G735 2006
248.8'45—dc22
                                                                                    2006022298

Printed in the United States of America

07 08 09 10 11 12 13 14 15 / LB-CF / 10 9 8 7 6 5 4 3 2

This book is dedicated to my wife, Jan, who has tolerated and uplifted me for 36 years, has made things happen in the lives of so many families and teens, and has given of herself tirelessly to our ministry with people.

Acknowledgments

With special thanks:

To my wife, Jan, for her heart for kids and families, and for her willingness to do what it takes to speak truth into people's lives.

To my daughter and son-in-law, Melissa and Blake Nelson, whom I have the pleasure to work alongside at Heartlight, and my son Adam, who grew up at Heartlight. All three have helped me make this ministry what it is today.

To Paul and Ann Kelsey, for their support and generosity while I wrote this book, and for ensuring that you would be able to hold it in your hand.

To James Lambert of Shoreline Management, for his oversight, wisdom, and help in making this book a reality.

To Brian Luwis of America World Adoption, for his friendship and commitment to excellence in his work with orphans around the world.

To all the Harvest House folks, including Bob Hawkins, Carolyn McCready, and Terry Glaspey, who have involved themselves in this project to ensure that families struggling with their teens might find hope and direction through this resource.

To Heartlight Ministries board members Bill and Susanne Walsh, Jim and Lynn Samis, Bill and Elise Daniel, Mike and Dianne Puls, Dave and Brenda Herrmann, and Larry and Debra Frase, who serve kids and families throughout the U.S. by their commitment to ensure that those who struggle have a place to go to in times of need.

To Bill O'Connell, Mac and Maria Slingerlend, and Tom and Lou Ann Nisbett, Freddie Albaugh, John and Mary Nice, Paul and Kelly Gittemeier, Dr. Charlie Wilson, Dale Poole, Jeff Sieh, Keith Hill, and the Heartlight Community, for their constant support, unfailing friendship, and commitment to Jan, me, and to our work with teens and families.

To Amanda Childress, my assistant, who gives of herself endlessly, fulfilling Heartlight's mission to struggling families through all of our outreach programs and resources.

To all the staff at Heartlight, for your commitment to teens and families, and for inviting these people into your lives. It is a joy to serve alongside each of you.

To Rick Dunham, Marissa Mathews, and Trent Dunham of Dunham + Company, who have inspired our staff and helped Heartlight flourish.

To my mom and dad—Pat and Dale Gregston—and to Joe Mooberry, Clifton Taulbert, Joe White, Richard Beach, Steve Hubachek, and Billy Sprague, for all the lessons you have taught me. I'm amazed at how much wiser you all have become as I have grown older.

To my two granddaughters, Maile and Macie, who make me laugh and relax, and who constantly remind me of the preciousness of all my children.

CONTENTS

Foreword 9

Introduction 11

1. Hope amid the Conflict 15

2. Don't Lose Hope 27

3. Understanding and Wisdom 33

4. Were My Parents Really That Bad? 43

5. The Problem of Performance-Based Relationships 53

6. Why Does My Child Act This Way? 63

7. The Importance of Pain 79

8. Loss 95

9. Putting Your Knowledge to Work 109

10. The Importance of a Belief System 125

11. Setting Boundaries 141

12. Allowing Your Child to Be in Control 157

13. Building Maturity by Giving Responsibility 171

14. We're Spinning out of Control 183

15. Hope in a Difficult Time 195

16. Where Are They Now? 205

Notes 213

FOREWORD

I first shook the hand of a young man named Mark Gregston in 1981. He had just stepped on the campus of our Kanakuk Kamp to introduce himself as the new Young Life leader for our little town of Branson, Missouri.

Little did I know what great friends we would become—and the phenomenal impact he would have over the coming years on the lives of thousands of teenage kids. In fact, in all my years of working with kids—seeing 20,000 a year pass through our Kanakuk Kamp programs—I don't know many men who have made a greater impact on the world of struggling teens.

With more than 30 years of experience working with children and parents who find themselves struggling through the teen years, Mark has become a true expert in understanding the unique challenges facing teens and their families. And he understands so well how to advise parents who are navigating those often rough waters of adolescence.

The Heartlight residential program for struggling teens that he and his beautiful wife, Jan, began 20 years ago is extremely effective. Hundreds of troubled kids have graduated from that program over the years and have become not only successful adults but beautiful Christian men and women.

I have had a chance to meet the moms and dads of some of these kids. They are profoundly grateful for Mark and the skills he built into their lives so they could become the parents they so desperately wanted to be.

Mark refuses to pull any punches or sidestep any sticky or difficult situations, as you will quickly find out in the pages of this book. He speaks directly to the issues confronting parents and teens in this day and provides solid biblical and practical help while sharing his own mistakes, hurts, and struggles.

His heart for helping parents and teens will also become evident very quickly as you read this book. You will see that he has spent countless hours in the trenches with thousands of struggling families, committed to remaining there until they are able to get on the other side of their struggle.

While most people his age are trying to find ways to slow down and retire, Mark is constantly searching for new and better ways to meet the needs of parents and families. And this book does just that. I can guarantee that if you are wrestling with how to parent your teen or going through a crisis with your child, or if you have a child about to enter those difficult years, this book is for you!

Joe White
President, Kanakuk Kamps
Branson, Missouri

Introduction

The world your kids live in today is a mess. As they move into their teen years, they face unimaginable pressure to turn away from the values you have worked so hard to instill into their lives. Their world is different from the one you and I grew up in. Parenting teens during this time requires a different style of parenting than most parents are used to.

Regardless of how good a parent you are, certain forces are at work to send your kids spinning off in a direction you could never imagine.

In more than 30 years of working with troubled teens, I have seen parent after parent wonder what in the world happened. They seemed to wake up one morning and discover their teens had completely changed. Loving, kind, and thoughtful kids had turned into people they didn't even know. No wonder many parents are scared and unprepared for the adolescent years ahead.

Perhaps that's the way you feel today.

Sure, you've built hedges around your kids. You've tried to raise them God's way. You've taught them to just say no. You've prayed together so you would stay together. You've had devotions. You've attempted to raise godly children in an ungodly world.

You've homeschooled, held ceremonies for your boy to become a man, told your girls that true love waits, and taken them to church, camps, and mission projects. But what you thought you could keep from happening—and what you had hoped would never happen—is not just knocking on your doorstep; it has opened the door and entered your home.

So now what?

First, let me give you a word of hope. You are not alone. Thousands of Christian parents across the country are struggling with their teens. They feel lost and are looking for ways to counteract the effects today's teen culture has on their children.

Friend, the Christian family is not immune to the negative effects of this world! It is susceptible to what every Christian parent has worked so hard to prevent. Parenting has no guarantees!

I quickly learned that lesson years ago when working as a Young Life leader. I saw patterns repeat themselves during the years I served as a youth minister and through 25 years of having teens live with us in a residential counseling setting. These experiences have helped me understand the vastness of the need and the depth of the difficulties parents face today. In fact, that's what led me and my wife to start the Heartlight program in the late 1980s—and what has kept us going after working with more than 1500 young people and their families in that program.

I guarantee you that you can have hope. That's the reason for this book. I also want to reassure you that you can find a way through your kids' difficult teen years. Navigating these waters is going to take some work, but it's worth it. And you should know that getting your children through these difficult times is going to be as much about you as it is about them.

The good news is that you *can* get to the other side of these adolescent years. And if your relationship with your child is broken, you can restore it.

My desire is to unpack for you what I have learned during the years I have worked with troubled teens and their families. I want to show you how to deal with your teen and give you hope, direction, and insight whether you are in a crisis situation today or you want to prevent such a day in the future.

May God use this book to enlighten, empower, and encourage you in one of the greatest challenges you will ever face—parenting your teen.

CHAPTER ONE

HOPE AMID
THE CONFLICT

You are probably opening this book because you are dealing with disappointment regarding your child. You may also feel abandoned by friends and God and be tempted to despair because you're not exactly where you'd thought you'd be as a parent. You might be asking questions like these:

- How did I end up in the very place that I have worked so hard to avoid?
- Why is my child so angry? We've given her everything.
- How could we have done everything so right and have everything end up so wrong?
- Why is my child making the choices she is?
- Why does my child hate me? I have done nothing but love him.
- How could something so well-intentioned turn out so bad?
- Who is this child that woke up this morning?
- Why is my family falling apart? We've worked so hard to keep it together.

You desperately need something right now—an expectation, trust, a wish, something to look forward to, an aspiration, or hope. Especially when your relationship with your child seems to be falling apart.

Watching your child go through difficult times and cause conflict and disruption in your household is one of the worst tragedies you can face. It will move you to thinking things you never thought you'd think. When a desire you have for your child (and perhaps for yourself) vanishes, the pain can be indescribable.

You're probably ready for anything that will give you even a glimmer of hope. Perhaps you long to hear that you can turn around the crisis at hand.

I pray that in the following pages you will find hope and encouragement and that you will learn how to deal effectively with your struggling child or prepare for the potentially difficult years ahead.

Reality Check

The process starts with a reality check. It is simply this: Every parent struggles. If you haven't, you will. If you are struggling now, you can find hope.

I've sat with thousands of parents who, like you, are trying to understand just what is happening with their families. They are confused and distraught by their children's behavior and choices. They want to know what to do, and they want to know if they have any reason to hope for their family's future.

Not long ago I had just such a meeting with a dad. He sat across from me at a conference table, and with tears in his eyes, a broken heart, and desperation in his words, he said, "Mark, just tell me there's hope for my daughter."

You are not alone!

If you have ever seen *Fiddler on the Roof,* you will remember Tevye, the father. Tevye struggled with his youngest daughter, Chava, who made some choices against Tevye's will. In the play, Tevye sings a song called the "Chava Ballet Sequence," which he directed to his youngest daughter, his little bird, showing his frustration and despair. I still tear up when I hear this song. The song pictures a father letting go and reflecting on his daughter with great disappointment.

> *Little Bird, Little Chavaleh,*
> *I don't understand what's happening today.*
> *Everything is all a blur...*
> *Gentle and kind and affectionate,*
> *The sweet little bird you were,*
> *Chavaleh, Chavaleh.*[1]

Perhaps you've gone through a difficult time with your child, and you're trying to figure out what just happened. Or perhaps you're in the midst of that confusion right now, and you wonder if you'll ever make it to the other side. Or maybe you see something coming, and you want to prepare yourself.

Whatever your situation, you need to understand another reality. God hasn't abandoned you. In all the confusion and darkness, He is still there. His promises of turning ashes into beauty, sadness into joy, and mourning into dancing are not just phrases of Scripture that reflect His power and show His ability. They are promises for people in dark times. They are for parents of teens who are struggling through things they never expected.

Could God be absent? Would He be absent? Not on your life.

Hopelessness or Opportunity?

Hopelessness feels like a dark tunnel with no end. But add God to the picture, and everything changes. Your seemingly hopeless situation could possibly be one of the greatest opportunities for you and your child to connect in ways far beyond anything you ever dreamed possible.

Over and over again I have seen parents and their struggling teens travel down the road of life together. As the load lightens, they have found hope in the darkness. And they have learned things about themselves and each other that they could not have learned any other way. The same can happen for you.

This dark chasm you're in will not last forever. This time is but a chapter in your life's story. Don't look for a quick fix, and don't expect to find any timetable except God's.

As Albert Einstein once said, "The reason for time is so that everything doesn't happen at once." Your family's healing won't happen at once. It will be a journey. But you will get to the other side.

To the dad I mentioned earlier who asked me if there was hope for his daughter, my answer was yes. And that is my answer to you today too. You can have hope for your relationship with your child. But the answer isn't going to come on the timetable that you think it will. It won't look anything like you think it will look, and someday you'll be amazed at how much better your relationship is with your child.

The Bigger Picture

Whenever I talk with parents of a child who is out of control, they want to know three things:

"Why is this happening?"

"Why is my child doing this?"

"What do I need to do (or be) to help my child?"

These are good questions that need to be asked and need to be answered. But those answers can only come when you begin to understand God's intent and purpose for families.

The reasons why teens struggle are obvious when something has gone terribly wrong in their lives—rape, sexual abuse, death, divorce damage, or other tragedies. But when everything a parent has done has been well-intentioned and no obvious trauma has caused a child to spin out of control, parents can naturally wonder why all this is happening, question their worthiness as parents, or believe they are being punished for something.

Parents are not generally prepared to handle the crisis of an out-of-control teen because they believe their parenting skills have made their children impregnable to the stuff of life all around them. They believe their children will never make any poor choices and that God seems to be protecting their children more than other children.

Consequently, they haven't developed any skills to handle crises.

A young father approached me in Los Angeles a couple of years ago and asked what I thought about a program called Growing Kids God's Way (I get asked this quite a bit). I'm sure this is a good program for some kids, but it hasn't been for the type of teens I am involved with. I shared that I didn't really know much about the program but that several of the families who had placed kids with us had tried this approach.

He went on to say that if the parents of the kids in our residential program had used this approach, they evidently did a poor job, or they wouldn't have ended up needing that kind of help. As the hair on my neck began to bristle, I told him I would have to disagree with his statement because parents at Heartlight are some of the neatest people I've ever met, and they have loved their kids and done everything possible to resolve the issues that their children were going through.

He replied, "Well, my kids will never end up there [at Heartlight]. It just won't happen," inferring that either he possesses all that his kids will ever need or that his kids would never make bad choices or experience any trauma.

I responded that I hoped that he was right, that his kids would never need the services of the Heartlight residential program and that he would never have to go through struggles with his children.

But this father's arrogant mind-set is the type of thinking that usually gets parents into trouble. Anyone can have a struggling teen, regardless of how good they are at being parents. This understanding will save you a lot of grief! And you just might prevent your child from going down a path no one would want to walk.

Parents also face the challenge of guiding kids through the various stages of life. The mind-set and skills you possessed during your children's preteen years, when parents can do no wrong, life is simpler, and kids enjoy and depend on parents more, may have worked well for you. But as your child ages and begins adolescence, you too will need to change. For instance, kids' thinking switches from concrete to abstract, the opposite sex becomes important, they begin to exercise more freedom, social circles enlarge, and their learning style changes.

Lecture must move to discussion. A parent's main role changes from a protector to a preparer. A parent who has never before had to admit wrongdoing might now have to confess his or her shortcomings.

On top of this, through experience and failure, parents begin to learn how to handle the personal difficulties teens experience. All of this can be overwhelming and emotionally draining. Hope can never come at a better time.

Embrace the Journey

Kids live in a confusing world. We must stay the course in loving and preparing our teens and understand they are on a journey to adulthood. We can embrace the journey they are on by learning some new skills, understanding their world, and discerning the hand of God on their lives. As we give them the freedom to experience this journey, we will ultimately foster more authentic relationships with them and allow them to grow personally.

Ursula K. Le Guin, an American author, wrote, "It is good to have an end to journey towards; but it is the journey that matters, in the end."[2] From where you stand, the journey may appear to be going nowhere. But it could be the greatest journey that you and your child will ever experience together. It won't look like what you always thought it would, and it probably won't follow the path you dreamed and hoped you would get to walk.

This struggle has come to your family for a reason. You're the parent of *this* child for a reason. The timing is not accidental. You probably don't understand all the reasons for these struggles, but that doesn't diminish their purpose or the plan behind them. They are part of the journey God has for you and your child. And He'll use it all. Regardless of how hard the circumstances may be and how devastating the issues are, nothing comes to you that hasn't first passed through God's hands. And that which does come, comes to transform you more into His image so He can use you in a greater way for His purpose.

Rick Warren has stated in his book *The Purpose-Driven Life,* "It's not about you."[3] This statement helps define our purpose in life. But regarding your current family crisis, it *might* be about you. After all, the fruit doesn't fall far from the tree.

Is the hardship with your child actually about you? Could be. Is it about your child? I'm sure it is. Is it about your family? Absolutely. Is it about God? You can bet your life on it.

My point is this: The child you brought home many years ago with God's thumbprint on his or her life is the same child today. Just because this child is struggling doesn't mean this child's Maker or purpose for being created has changed. If indeed this child was created for a purpose, as Scripture reminds us, then that purpose is not being sidetracked just because of a few bumps in the road (regardless of how big they might appear). God just might use these bumps to transform your child into a vessel that He can better use for the purpose for which he or she was created.

Please don't hear me say that God caused all that is happening. That's a completely different discussion. But I promise you this: He'll use whatever's happening in your life and your child's life for good things in the future. Just because you can't see them now doesn't mean they aren't coming. God is leading you in the journey.

I can tell you from my experience with families that short of your child or you dying, you will get on the other side of this time. But the way you get there—the path you chose to follow—will determine the length of time your child stays in darkness and the quality of relationship that you share during the struggle.

For years (most of my life) I've been quietly disgruntled at all those people who have not given me what I wanted, have hurt or offended me, or have caused pain in my life. As I gray, I get this overwhelming sense that they'll all be standing with God as I get to heaven (assuming I'm the last to go) and God will say, "Mark, I want you to know that I used these people in your life to transform you more into My image and to prepare you for your work with those who were struggling."

This greater understanding has transformed the way I approach conflict and has allowed me to not be controlled by seemingly devastating events in my past. That same transformation is the right path for you to take on your journey with your child today.

A young lady asked me not long ago, "What's the worst thing that's ever happened in your life?" My answer after a little reflection was this: There is no worst thing. I now see how God has used each of those miserable dark times in my life, and I would never want to give up the lessons I've learned or the good that has come out of each incident, happening, or situation. This perspective changes the way that I see everything, and it will change the way you view your child, his or her struggles, and the pain your family is experiencing.

True Stories

Throughout this book I'll tell stories about different kids who have lived with us and their families. We all learn from mistakes others have made, and through their stories we can find answers to those unanswered questions and find hope in some pretty dark times. Before we jump into the next chapter, let me introduce you to five of these kids. Perhaps one of these young people resembles your child and pictures what you are experiencing.

Gracie

Gracie's parents were committed to protecting their child from "the world," dedicated to spending as much time with her as possible during her forming years, and devoted to teaching her a Christian curriculum for homeschooling. An honorable, well-intentioned, thought-out track. A great relationship ensued, Gracie benefited from a good curriculum, and she developed a good sense of security. She was outstanding at her church and an excellent athlete.

As she entered adolescence, her parents wanted her to become more socially exposed. They allowed her to start public school in the ninth grade. The result was a mess. Because she had not integrated with her peers, she went to extremes to fit in, becoming sexually active within months of going to school and drinking from dares of her peers. Within six months her language was terrible, her demeanor hateful, and her love for God diminished. Her family's worst fears had materialized, and their loving beautiful daughter had turned dark and vulgar.

Michael

Michael's parents knew since he was two years old that something wasn't quite right. He was always different. Always in trouble. Always an outcast. Always at odds with other kids and teachers. Regardless of the punishment he received or the consequences he experienced, Michael was always pushing the edge, stepping over the line most of the time.

As Michael entered adolescence he became enlightened to his awkwardness and began to use drugs and alcohol to self-medicate his relational pain. The drugs led to more and more poor choices that eliminated him from just about every positive activity that could affirm him. He was failing school. His family felt helpless and frustrated as they watched him deteriorate, spiraling into despondency.

Erica

Just one of those normal kids, involved in everything and loved by everyone, Erica was the pride of all—her teachers, her family, her church, and her coaches. She had an intriguing and attractive personality and a witty intellect. Her love for the Lord was encouraging, her love for her family heartening. Her parents were involved in the church and required that she be also, participating in everything and involved every time the church doors were open.

Then one morning, as her parents say, she woke up and was a completely different person. Everything changed, and not just a little. She changed drastically. A few months later her parents found out she was being sexually molested by their church's youth minister.

Brian

Brian was adopted from another country. About a year after the adoption, when he was four, they realized they had adopted a mess. Nothing seemed to work. He wouldn't bond with his parents. There was always some distance. The doctors called it attachment disorder; his parents called it disappointment and hurt. Never had something so well-intentioned gone so bad. Never a hug, never a response, always wanting to be left alone. When he came to us, his connection to life began through a horse named Mariah.

Alan

Alan was a typical attention deficit kid, always bouncing around to different things. His intellect made Alan capable of anything. He dove headfirst into everything he did, running 100 miles an hour. When he played baseball, he was the best, but his career was short-lived. When he played the guitar, he wowed people with his talent, but only momentarily. When he decided to become a Skinhead, he scared his family, but only temporarily. When he rode and roped on horseback, he was daring and magnificent, but fleeting at best. The low point came when his dad and he had it out, and in the resulting argument, his dad moved some of Alan's belongings to the front yard.

Alan ran into the house, and with a hammer began beating up the house, breaking and destroying his parent's belongings and their home. When Alan's father called the police, Alan ran upstairs and swallowed a bottle of pills. After he was admitted to the adolescent psych ward at a local hospital, his father called me. I met Alan and realized this was a lovable kid who wanted good things but didn't know how to get them.

Any of these stories sound familiar? Perhaps they, like other stories in this book, are being replicated in your home today. Let me assure you that if they are, they are not above God's reach or His concern. Nothing is. Your child is still the same child you brought home from the hospital nursery with excitement and joy. Your child is still the same bubbly child that used to make you laugh and make your heart jump for joy. Your child is still the same one you have poured your life into. He may be going through a difficult time, but he's still that same child, and your investment of time and effort has not been lost. She may seem like a completely different person, but she's not. And God has not abandoned you. Your family can survive and grow through your teen's struggles.

Working through this difficult time with your child is not an easy task. But it will be worth the effort. It may not look the way that you had planned or feel the way you always hoped it would be, but you just might be surprised on the other side of this hardship when you see that God has indeed been involved the whole journey, moving you and your child to a better place than you ever dreamed of.

CHAPTER TWO

DON'T LOSE HOPE

Each of the young people in the previous chapter—Gracie, Michael, Erica, Brian, and Alan—and their families experienced a situation that was very different from the others'. Each was dealing with very unique issues and family backgrounds.

But something is very similar about each. And that similarity is this: Each family identified a problem. None of them disengaged from their children. They moved toward their children to help and didn't allow their children's behavior to control them or detract from their love for their children.

They worked to understand their children and became part of the process of healing rather than fighting against their child. And they offered hope to their children, a hope of a restored relationship and a hope of getting through the tough times regardless of what happened.

Working through the struggle with their child led to a deeper relationship with their child, and all of them developed deeper understandings of God, His grace, and His plan for their lives. In each situation, the parents maintained a relationship with their child and were willing to tackle the hard stuff. Consequently, they validated what they instilled in their child in their earlier years.

In nearly every case, the process ended up better than the parents thought it would. Why? Because the young people I know want to know that their parents—who have stood with them while all was going well—will stand with them now that things aren't going so well. In other words, teens wonder, *It's easy to love me when I'm behaving the way you want me to, but will you still love me when I don't?* Good question.

My wife was sexually abused as a child. It's a terrible story that lasted seven years. But with the support of her family, our family, and friends around her, Jan got to the other side of it. And though it was awful and messed Jan up for years, those who loved her stood with her, and she was able to overcome the trauma and become a beautiful woman of God.

Amazingly, the very things I love most about Jan are those characteristics, attitudes, and unique personality traits that have developed in her because of the abuse. The things I love the most came out of that which I hated the most. Paul wasn't kidding when he wrote that God can make "all things work together for good…" (Romans 8:28 NKJV).

True Hope

I wish I could tell you that every one of the kids I mentioned in the last chapter is doing well now. That would be false hope. I also wish I could tell you that in only a few months, things will turn around, and your child will stop messing up. But that would also be a false hope. And I wish I could assure you that your child's struggles are just momentary. But once again, that would be a false hope.

Now, each one of those may happen. But that should not be the basis of your hope. Why? Because our hope is not in anyone's behavior or the timing of our struggles. That's why the only hope that I can impart is this: God is involved in your situation. Our hope is in God. Even though your child is going through a tough time, God has not somehow left you, ignored your family, or neglected you.

Let me remind you that Scripture tells us in Proverbs 16:9 that a man's heart plans his way, but God directs his steps. God is with you every step of the way! And remember Jeremiah 29:11: " 'For I know the plans I have for you,' declares the LORD, 'plans to prosper you and not to harm you, plans to give you hope and a future.' "

As a parent you need to grasp this truth: God's plan for your family is not thwarted because of your child's choices or because your plan isn't working. He's still directing your family's path, and His plans for you are still His plans for you. Could He have chosen you to be part of a process that He will use to bring about greater things than you could ever imagine for your child?

A New Perspective

We recently remodeled our home. A project that was to last 3 months lasted nearly 18 months, and costs exceeded projections by more than 50 percent. Throughout the project we met workers that I now consider friends. They are people I admire, feel blessed to have been with, and have enjoyed in our long task.

But amid the trials of the remodel, others took advantage of us. They lied to us, conned us, made horrendous mistakes, broke promises, and caused much pain and hardship. Jan and I asked ourselves questions throughout the project: "Why in the world is this happening this way?" "I thought we had done everything right…didn't we?" "How can people ignore all that we've lined out for them?" "Why has something that was supposed to be so easy become so hard?" Sound familiar?

Then Jan and I realized what God was doing. Years ago, we prayed to be involved in the lives of people who were struggling. And once again God was honoring our prayers, bringing these struggling people to us. And He didn't just bring the ones we wanted, but He brought others to us we would never expect. And He'll continue to bring those people into our lives at our expense.

A word to the wise. Be careful what you pray for.

In our remodel project, what I thought was an inconvenience was really an opportunity. What I thought was wrong was an opportunity to share what was right. And what I thought was unfair really isn't that big of a deal now. And the house? It looks better than I thought it would. I have learned again that when you arrive on the other side of any issue, the issue looks smaller, and the promises of God remain true. He amazes me, and He amazes me the most when opportunity is born out of confusion and struggle.

Maybe your relationship with your child feels like my home remodeling project. Perhaps what you thought would be a momentary struggle has turned into a long-term battle. If so, I want to challenge you to a different perspective: Conflict and struggle bring about changes.

As a parent of a teen who is struggling, you have undoubtedly prayed for God to help you become the parent He has called you to be. Well, that's just what He's doing now! See this time as a tremendous opportunity to build into your child's life, trusting God to direct your path along the way. Now's your chance to be used at a time when you're needed the most. Don't back off from the role He's called you to, the role you have been practicing for all your life. Develop a mind-set that is consistent with God's—that He has your child's life planned out—so you'll be able to develop a deeper relationship with your child during this difficult time and shorten the amount of time that your child remains in darkness.

Your perspective of what is happening within your family is key. Your correct understanding of your role is necessary. Your willingness to hang in there during this tough time demonstrates perseverance at its best. Your commitment to be a part of God's plan for your child, seen or unseen, is godly. Loving your child in difficult times shows your true love. Your knowledge that God is involved in your family is an anchor of hope that will keep you reflecting His love to your child.

If you will keep this perspective, you can have genuine hope that your child can get on the other side, and your relationship can be restored.

The Path to Restoration

Even though your heart cries today for your relationship with your child to be restored, restoration takes a little work and is rarely an easy process. In fact, it takes a committed, unwavering perseverance. Scripture tells us in Galatians 6:9, "Let us not become weary in doing good, for at the proper time we will reap a harvest if we do not give up." So don't give up.

And keep a proper frame of mind. When you begin to think about your child and what he or she has been involved in behaviorally, it's usually worse than what you think but never quite as bad as you can imagine. Every difficulty can be overcome, and every relationship can be restored.

Another key to a proper frame of mind is to understand that what is happening right now is not the whole story. The whole story is what God is up to, which entails a whole lot more people than you or your child and a schedule that reaches far beyond your own.

Finally, don't panic. You probably feel alone in this whole mess. But just because people are silent doesn't mean other families don't struggle. Remember, everyone struggles at some time.

I have discovered that parents usually get pretty scared when a child begins to struggle. Moms have a tendency to get emotional and want to fix things, and dads have a tendency to walk away as if their inability to fix everything is a sign of their lack of manhood. Parents may feel inadequately prepared to tackle these new challenges. They may have unresolved issues in their own lives. A child could be bringing old skeletons out of the family closet. The struggle is just more than some parents feel they can handle, and they are exhausted.

Inadequacy, new challenges, unresolved issues, old skeletons, exhaustion—that list would scare anyone! This might be a good time to place these things in God's hands, trusting that He will cause all things to work together for good. If you do, you will be on the path to restoration.

The only true hope is that God is involved in what is going on with your child. His plan is not determined by what I or my child can or can't see. You and I know of God's hand in the past, and we know of it in the future, but our difficulty comes in believing in His involvement in what is happening today. Just remember what C.S. Lewis once said: "We're not necessarily doubting that God will do the best for us; we are wondering how painful the best will turn out to be."

CHAPTER THREE

Understanding and Wisdom

A s you begin dealing with a struggling teen, you immediately realize the need for understanding and wisdom. Let's consider a few of the basics that will be foundational as you build on your relationship with your teen.

Face the Right Direction

The old Chinese proverb tells us that the journey of a thousand miles begins with a single step. I would add that you might want to make sure you're facing the right direction.

Sadly, too many parents today move the wrong direction with their children. And they are exhausted. If you are already tired and feeling abandoned by a child who is struggling, you certainly don't want to be lost as well. As with any journey, a little bit of planning ensures you will get to the right destination. And the first priority is to make sure you're pointed in the right direction: loving your child, focusing on him or her, discerning what God may be doing, and avoiding condemnation.

During my years of involvement in Young Life (an organization that reaches out to lost teens) I told gospel stories every week. One of the stories that always caught my attention in a special way was of the woman caught in adultery in John 8. I always wondered what Jesus was writing in the sand when the crowd of religious leaders stood around her condemning her.

You'll probably remember that when the Pharisees brought the young girl to Jesus, they told Him they had caught her in adultery and that the law required them to stone her. They then asked Him what He would do. His response was to stoop down and write in the sand. Then He stood up and said, "He who is without sin among you, let him be the first to throw a stone at her" (John 8:7). Then Jesus stooped back down and began writing again. He wrote twice. I think I know what He wrote.

We obviously don't know for sure, but I bet He scribbled two simple and intriguing words the first time he wrote in the sand: What if. Those two words could hold anyone's interest for just a minute. After He wrote the words, capturing everyone's attention, He stood up, stated His decision, and then returned to writing on the ground.

The second time He stooped to write, I think He finished His question: What if...this was your daughter? At His spoken word, the rocks hit the ground. And with His sand-scribbled words, the jaws of every father in the crowd dropped as well. They probably also dropped their pride as they shuffled away, struggling to hold back the tears welling beneath their brow.

People always ask if this is true, if these were really the words Jesus wrote. And they ask if this woman was really a young girl. I don't know, but that's my gut feeling as I've read the story hundreds of times and seen the scenario between fathers and daughters just as often. Young girls freeze when confronted; older girls run. This girl stood there long enough for Jesus to share His liberating declaration.

Scripture says that the older men left the area first, followed by the younger men. Some say the older men left first because they recognized their own sinfulness. I wonder if it was also because many of them were dads. As the younger men followed, they may have asked, "What'd He say back there?" "Why are you so quiet?" "Did I just miss something?" You bet they did.

Seeing your child in a traumatic situation like that can get you facing the right direction. It can move your heart toward someone in your family who is struggling. I know from personal experience—a painful personal experience with my son.

Adam

My son, Adam, made a terrible mistake. He fell in love with a girl. The problem was, he was already married to another girl whom we had welcomed into our family a year prior. The divorce was finalized close to their second anniversary. Adam's decision closed the door to a lifetime with a daughter-in-law every father would ever want. The entire experience was painful, it hurt, and it tempted me to move to condemnation.

I was shocked that this could be happening to me and my wife, angered that my son would pull such a stunt, and infuriated over his timing. Didn't he realize how this would impact his and her families? And needless to say, I was embarrassed over his actions. I had performed the wedding and had spent quite a bit of time with her family. They loved my son, could say nothing wrong about him, and were excited about this new union. And when Adam betrayed that trust, the perfect son-in-law turned into a stranger who violated any integrity he might have possessed.

Having a son offend so many people was a whole new experience for me! Never had such pride turned to instant embarrassment. I had never felt the need to avoid some people, hoping they wouldn't ask. And I had never been so confused by a child's actions. I began to feel hurt and violated, feelings I've rarely felt.

I had always told Adam that he could never do anything to cause me to love him less. Now that was feeling a little shaky.

I was amazed how I felt so lost in the situation. But at the same time, I felt an overwhelming urge to pray for guidance, to seek wisdom, and to see with the eyes of my heart. I quietly stayed "misplaced" for a while, realizing as each day passed that regardless of how much control I have over my life, I have no control over some things. So instead of focusing on what I didn't have, I began asking how God might use me in the midst of this disaster.

My son would continue to be my son. And, as painful as it was, his father would continue to be his dad. Our situation taught me in a whole new way that those statements are more easily said than done, and no family is immune from such a struggle. Not mine. Not yours.

I find it intriguing that immediately after the story of the woman caught in adultery, Jesus said this: "I am the Light of the world; he who follows me will not walk in the darkness, but will have the Light of life" (John 8:12). I would have to say if that young woman's dad was indeed in that crowd, Jesus' comment was probably directed to him. That dad would have just encountered his child's sin and would have been living in that darkness that only a sinful child can bring. He needed the Light.

My world was not impregnable, and neither is yours. This kind of situation can happen to you, to those you love, and to those you know, regardless of how much you believe otherwise. This side of heaven, no family or child is immune to struggle.

Realize Grasping the Truth Isn't Easy

When a child struggles—and you accept that this can happen to your child—the way you look at just about everything changes. Embracing the truth in this time is not an easy thing. But if you will, your perspective changes. You realize that your child or your family never were really perfect. Your child's adolescent years tend to bring out some hidden imperfections.

Realizing that things aren't as right as you once thought will help you move from judgment to compassion and from harshness to tenderness.

Over the years, I have seen that when parents admit problems exist within their own families, they often change the way they handle situations. They react in a kinder, gentler, and compassionate way.

Embracing the truth is not easy. It can be downright hard. But when you admit and accept what is happening within your family, you have taken a major step toward your family's healing. American psychologist and philosopher William James said it this way: "Acceptance of what happened is the first step to overcoming the consequence of any misfortune." Here are some families that came to their realizations in different ways.

John and Virginia

John and Virginia had always strived for good things for their two daughters. They lived for their kids and were dedicated to being involved in all their activities. You could always find them at church, giving their kids everything.

Laughter filled the house. Holidays were great. Vacations were wonderful. And pictures throughout the house reflected the depth of the relationships in this family. Everyone in Phoenix knew them as a perfect family.

But John called me late one night. His first words to me quivered as they came out of his mouth. "Mark, it's worse than I thought."

Patty, their 17-year-old daughter, had come home from a night out high from smoking pot. And during her stupor she shared with them how she had been doing this for a couple years, and they could do nothing about it. I listened as he shared what was clearly a double dose of bad news. The first dose was the initial shock that their daughter even knew what pot was and that she was smoking it. The second was that this activity had been going on for quite some time. His words to me were filled with hopelessness, and my responses to him filled my eyes with tears. Rarely does a father feel as he did.

John's difficult realization came as a *shock*.

Pete and Jennifer

Pete and Jennifer called and asked if they could meet with me. I had met with them off and on during the past year. They kept me informed about their son, Kyle. They started the conversation with "Well, we want to let you know what has been happening, catch you up, and get some advice."

I heard that within the past week, their son had smoked dope in his room, had a tirade with his mother in the car and called her every name in the book, had threatened to leave home, and wanted to drop out of school. For months I had listened to them describing the ongoing saga with their son, but they never followed any advice or directive. When they finally asked what I thought, I decided the time had come to wake them up to what was going on. I had won the right to be heard as we had spent quite a bit of time together, and now was the time to bring some light to a dark subject.

I shared that I had seen their son deteriorate during the past ten months. A kid who was struggling through some normal teen issues had become a child who was brash enough to smoke dope in his parents' home, was depressed, had wrecked two cars, had been arrested three times, had lost two jobs, was now flunking school, was yelling and screaming at all the family, and had turned into a vulgar and hateful young man. If they didn't wake up and do something quickly, their son would soon be dead.

As difficult as this was to hear, Pete and Jennifer both broke down crying as their eyes were opened by someone who could give them perspective. They didn't want to see the truth because it would reveal that they had failed somewhere and that they didn't have a perfect child. Whereas John and Virginia's realization had come as a shock, Pete and Jennifer's realization came as *enlightenment*.

Steve and Tonia

Steve and Tonia adopted a little girl and a younger boy with high hopes for both. But with their adopted son, Adam, things were less than ideal. And as Adam began to act out, instead of experiencing consequences for inappropriate behavior, Adam received accolades and applause for anything good. Never confronting Adam's unacceptable behavior, Steve and Tonia believed in "powering him through" the struggles with encouragement to do better. Meanwhile, Adam's occasional visit to the principal's office upgraded to visits by the local police.

Steve and Tonia believed their son was so good that he wasn't capable of doing anything bad. This mentality allowed Adam to continue to violate just about every rule and boundary. As Adam's parents believed and lived the fantasy that their son could do no wrong, Adam plummeted in every area of his life—he could do no right. By minimizing the problems, they actually allowed them to grow.

I'm not sure what awakened Steve and Tonia. I remember Steve saying, "I can run a company of ten thousand people around the world, but I can't figure out how to help my only son, who lives in my own home." Adam paid the price for their blindness, and they eventually had to wake up to their responsibility for what they had not seen. Rather than a shock or an enlightenment, Steve and Tonia experienced an *awakening*.

Sam and Marty

Sarah was always a difficult kid. From the day Sam and Marty adopted her they knew something was different. She didn't connect with other kids. She was very bright in every way, but she couldn't stay out of trouble. Throughout grade school and junior high, she was always pushing the limits, always manipulating, never accepting responsibility, always having an excuse.

Sam and Marty inherited these issues. They had no control over them, and they weren't going to be able to correct or prevent Sarah's behaviors. Their love for Sarah was deep, and they soon realized that the "Sarah project" was going to last a long time, so they prepared as best they could. They moved from counselor to psychologist to psychiatrist with all sorts of testing. Rarely have I seen parents willing to do so much with so little return.

Sarah got in trouble at a church youth retreat for taking pills, and that was the straw that broke the camel's back. Sam and Marty felt that if they didn't get Sarah to a residential setting that could control her—and hopefully help in the process—she wouldn't reach her eighteenth birthday. Their realization of the problem was not a shock or awakening or enlightenment, it was a *validation* of what they already knew.

James and Laura

Tammy had always been the perfect child. Never in a million years would anyone imagine this young girl was struggling through some very dark issues. What had been kept secret for years had finally risen to the surface with Tammy's tearful confession of being sexually abused by an uncle.

Feeling angry and violated, James and Laura struggled with a confusing set of emotions and beliefs. They loved Tammy, but they burned with anger at the once trusted family member. They privately beat themselves up over and over, hoping to find solace but really trying to convince themselves that they had done everything possible to protect their child.

Their realization of their child's problems and struggles came through *exposure*. Exposure to something new and foreign. They went to sleep in one world with a joyful thankfulness for their daughter and awoke the next day in a world of confusion and bewilderment.

Shock, enlightenment, awakening, validation, exposure. Other parents come to the truth through an *acceptance* of what they already know but find hard to believe. Others through an eventual *agreement* as Mom and Dad finally agree that something is wrong, and something needs to be done to correct what is spinning out of control.

From Acceptance to Understanding

Regardless of how parents come to the realization that their teen is indeed struggling, the truth is never easy to accept. But as soon as most parents accept their plight, they want to understand what is happening. And they are driven to find answers and a solution to their predicament.

I've told people this a thousand times: After finding out the truth, you're in no worse place than you were before you knew it. You just know about it. Bad news is never fun to hear, but it gives you the opportunity to do something about it!

Understanding Can Change Your Perspective

This is such an important principle; let me illustrate it for you.

Let's say a man stumbles into a room where I'm giving a talk. His speech is slurred as he awkwardly moves towards me. As he falls down before me, he throws up all over my shoes. With garbled words, he struggles to tell me how sorry he is. He then passes out and falls on my feet.

Most people's first response would be that he's drunk, and someone ought to keep bums like this out of the room. Most onlookers would get angry. Others embarrassed. Some mad enough that they'd want to drag this drunk out back.

Then I tell you one small detail that might change the way you respond. He's having a brain aneurism. He's just displayed all the symptoms. And that one small point of understanding changes everything, changes your perspective, and moves you in ways that you would not have moved otherwise.

Because we now understand what is happening, we don't really care about him throwing up, and we don't really feel embarrassed. And the stench and the behavior don't bother us in the slightest. Matter of fact, we are moved to help in any way we can.

A woman is brought into an emergency room yelling and screaming at everyone, cussing like a sailor, and throwing obscenities at everyone present. Does it matter? Are we going to correct her? Are we going to not help her because she's offended someone? Not on your life. She has just broken her back in a car accident, and whatever she displays doesn't matter because so much more is at stake.

Both these situations are similar to teens' struggles. Their behavior isn't right, but the behavior is not the issue. It is a symptom of something greater. And when you understand that their behavior is a reflection of something larger, you will change the way you respond and offer yourself to them.

Understanding and wisdom help you to see with the eyes of your heart, to look beyond the surface, to discover that which is hidden and unseen.

One final word on understanding. I realize that our first response to the realization that our child is messing up is usually anger. Anger is an emotional response to not getting what you want. But as I tell most people, once you get beyond the fact that this isn't about you, and you allow your new understanding to captivate all your emotions, your heart will follow. A new understanding of your child will also bring a new sense of appreciation.

CHAPTER FOUR

WERE MY PARENTS REALLY THAT BAD?

How did you learn to be a parent?

You probably learned from your own parents. But the transfer is not just "like father, like son." The transfer is quite different from that. It's more like this: "What my dad did, I want to do differently." I used to think that I had to stand against everything he stood for. The generation gap was as big as the Grand Canyon.

I believe that is true for most of today's generation of parents. Most parents don't want to make the same mistakes they believe their parents made. Let me give you a very personal example.

My concept of discipline was formed from my childhood. If I did something against the rules, I was disciplined. That discipline was usually physical.

Pretty simple. Don't do anything bad, and you won't get nailed. If you did do something wrong, Dad would find out, get home from the office, and you'd get a few licks from the belt. Mom sold us out, and Dad corrected the problem. They probably learned the system from their parents, who were influenced by other military precedents.

I learned that you never said anything bad to your mom or dad. Cussing, swearing, and dirty jokes never darkened the doors of our home. Beds were always made. Shoes were always shined. You were always on time. So much was expected of us:

"Yes, Sir."

"No, Sir."

"Yes, Ma'am."

"No, Ma'am."

"Load up; we're going."

"Clean your plate."

"Comb your hair."

"Stand up straight."

"When you shake someone's hand, (the civilian act of a salute) do it firmly."

"Speak only when spoken to."

It was Dad's way or no way. Period. No sissy stuff. Treat a girl like a lady. Keep your closets and toys neat. Take care of your business. Defend yourself. Treat your mom nice.

Sound a little like the military? You bet it did. Respect ran high, but it was a little short on the relational side. And it was that shortcoming that began to form the parent I would become.

But as I got older I began to understand what made my dad the way he was. I realized that my dad worked hard at the same job for 38 years to provide for his family because that was the way he loved his family. And he demanded (strongly) because that was the way you were to live. You respected your elders because that's the way it was. Period.

As my dark hair lightens, I hear less, and my eyesight diminishes. But I find that wisdom comes easier, that I listen more, and I see more with the eyes of my heart. I understand more about my mom and dad, and I realize that things really weren't as bad as I thought they were while growing up.

I now realize that my dad worked hard because he grew up during the Depression, and he knew what it meant to have nothing. I've never experienced anything close to that. He left his junior year of high school to go fight a war in the South Pacific. I spent my junior year with my girlfriend (who later became my wife), swimming laps and growing hair.

And I now understand that his desire was to provide for his family and to protect all of us. He did both. Food was always on the table, a roof was always over our heads, and we never got attacked.

But when the '60s and '70s came along, we wanted a "whole lotta love." In fact, we sang, "all you need is love." We wanted everyone to "shower the people you love with love."

Our music expressed our longing for and new pilgrimage to relationships, something our parents struggled with. The concept of all holding hands, growing out long hair, and screaming "peace" during an Asian conflict was confusing for those dads like mine who expressed love in other ways.

My point is that we need to understand that our concepts about discipline are usually formed in our childhood. And we often react against those things we saw as negative, even though at the time we didn't see them that way.

How My Parents Changed My Parenting Style

So, because of the way I was raised and my reaction against much of what I didn't understand, my focus when I raised my kids was relationships, not provision and protection. The pendulum of my parenting swung to the other side.

In fact, I believe this generation of parents has fallen head over heels toward emphasizing relationships in parenting. Think about it. We're the Starbucks generation. We want to have a place to go sit and have a cup of coffee and talk. We want to go to a Cheers kind of place where everyone knows our name. And somehow, we are determined to have relationships with our kids in extraordinary ways.

- We embrace new tools of communication like cell phones, text messaging, e-mail…anything to connect with our kids.
- We give our kids things we never got.
- We do things with our kids our parents never did with us.

- We become taxi drivers, shuttling out kids everywhere to do so much of what we couldn't do.
- We become coaches.
- We work in boosters clubs.
- We teach Sunday school.
- We homeschool.
- We indulge.
- Fathers push strollers, change diapers, and forsake business deals to spend time with their children.

This generation of parents—for the most part—is revolving its family life around its kids with the goal of better relationships. And while that may be a significant improvement in some ways, it has also produced some things we didn't anticipate.

The Danger of Moving from Parents to Peers

We should applaud most parents of this generation for their desire to build relationships with their kids, but putting kids at the center of our world has created a pretty self-centered generation. In my work with kids, I have found that they're usually immature and unappreciative of all that other people have done for them. They want more—even when they've had everything given to them.

They're often disrespectful and quick to say inappropriate things to parents, teachers, and coaches. In fact, kids often say things that would have gotten me knocked halfway into next week when I was a teen.

They seldom show appreciation, are often demanding, usually want more, and are rarely satisfied. They can't seem to have enough or keep busy enough.

And amazingly, they're angry.

I don't need to go further. You get the picture. And though I know plenty of exceptions to everything I'm writing, we need to understand that as parents we've created an environment we didn't anticipate. And for the most part, we have a generation of kids for which we didn't prepare. And we now feel what our parents felt. Our kids are thumbing their noses at us just as we thumbed our noses at our parents.

Somewhere along the line we moved from being parents to being peers. And that's a very dangerous move, regardless of how well-intentioned it is.

Think about it for a moment. Barking out orders is pretty easy when we're the boss. Giving direction is simple when we're the director. Correcting someone is relatively painless when we've been placed in an authority position. But correcting a peer is far harder.

When we are peers to our kids, we stand on equal ground with them. This has the potential to create stronger relationships with our children, but it undermines our position of authority.

So the big question is this: How do we regain that position of authority while maintaining the relationships we have longed for and worked so hard to develop with our kids?

Can you do both? Can you exercise authority and at the same time build a strong relationship with your kids? You bet you can. In fact, as you pursue this balance in parenting, I believe you'll even learn to love your kids in a deeper way and develop an even stronger relationship with them.

How do you do that? You start by telling them, "As your parent, I will stand beside you and walk with you. But make no mistake; I will stand in front of you when I need to."

Discipline entails helping your child get to where he wants to be and at the same time keeping him from a place he doesn't want to be. Take a moment to think about that because it is simple yet profound.

To pull this kind of parenting off, you have to be strong when you need to be strong and tender when you need to be tender. It's not either/or; it's both/and. A healthy parent knows when to do one or the other and when not to do either.

This kind of balance not only makes you a better parent, it reflects the very character of God. In the book of Isaiah we are told that He is like a mighty warrior (Isaiah 42:13). Yet in that same book we read,

"As a mother comforts her child, so will I comfort you" (Isaiah 66:13 NIV).

God embraces both characteristics, feminine and masculine. He is a God of power and a God with a great sense of tenderness. If one of our purposes as parents is to give our kids a taste of the character of God, then we must be tough when we need to be and tender when that's appropriate.

If you've never been firm with your children, being tough with them will probably be difficult. But your kids desperately need this kind of parenting. You will never ultimately be successful if you are unable to set boundaries and be strong with your children.

On the other hand, if you've never been tender with your child, you need to start that today. Your kids will have a difficult time accepting your new desire for warmth and gentleness, but it's never too late to start.

Balance and Focus in Discipline

Many parents don't discipline their children because they're afraid they will become like that military father whom they swore they would never be like. Others don't discipline because they're afraid of losing something with their child that they have worked years to attain: a good relationship. Then there are those parents who flat don't know what to do because they think everything has gone so well. They can't imagine that their child could somehow do wrong. As a result, they could be blindsided when their child requires some behavioral changes, consequences, or boundaries.

Most parents are simply unprepared for the teen years. They don't easily move from the lecture method to the discussion method. They are reluctant to give their kids more freedom. They are surprised when they catch a glimpse of adolescent rebellion on occasion. They feel abandoned when their kids begin to move away from them socially.

At the core, the teenage years are a time of change. And you need to be prepared for that change. You need to understand the new world your teen moves into. If you do, you will be prepared, rather than being caught with your guard down.

Making that transition can be a real challenge. Raising our kids by doing everything for them is easy. And we enjoy knowing that for the most part, they think we can do no wrong. But as kids get older, things change, don't they? They go off to sixth or seventh grade and find that they aren't as cool as they thought they were. And as they move from concrete thinking to abstract thinking, they begin to view their parents differently as well. They begin to realize that Mom and Dad aren't as cool as they thought they were.

When that happens, things can get confusing as you parent your teen. For example, I am always amazed at how teens can turn an issue about them to an issue about you, pointing out the shortcomings in your life as a parent.

Let's make sure we are clear on this: Parents need to deal with some of their own issues, but discipline's focus is about the child, not the parent. (By the way, how you deal with your own issues will determine how effective you are in your discipline techniques. But your issues don't give license to your children, at any age, to ignore or neglect the type of discipline that will help them grow.)

Teen discipline should target dishonesty, disobedience, and disrespect. Your child should learn that these negative traits bring painful consequences. But the positive alternatives bring desirable results:

- Honesty will help them in their relationships in the future.
- Obedience will help them gain direction and insight into life.
- Respect is the bedrock of all friendships and interpersonal relationships.

Your correction of your children over these qualities is vital. And never let them try to make it about you. It is always about them. Your correction will help them have the type of relationships they really want, and it will keep them from destroying or impeding relationships with their foolishness.

I'll add one more note. I've always said that moms instill a sense of value in a child, and dads validate that sense of value. But I'm amazed to see how many times I see Mom being the only one doing all the discipline with Dad participating very little. Kids pick up one message from these dads: "I don't care." Without participation in the discipline of a child, a dad will force a child to find validation somewhere else.

The Importance of Discipline

I don't know of any parents who don't want to help their children grow into strong and mature adults. But if you think discipline is just punishment and the inflicting of pain, no wonder you don't want to be involved. Discipline is about building the character qualities of honesty, obedience, and respect, and I encourage you to embrace your wonderful leadership role in your child's life.

If you are currently struggling with the discipline of your child, I encourage you to hang in there. You will eventually get on the other side of this thing called adolescence. A brighter day is ahead. You can have a deeper relationship with your child than you had with your parents. So hang in there.

John Wayne once said, "Courage is being scared to death but saddling up anyway." It's getting back up in the saddle when you've been thrown for a loop. These are true words...especially understood by those of us who have ever broken or trained horses. The training process begins easy, but it can get pretty ugly.

I have a set practice for breaking and training horses, but I adapt it to each one. And the course of action I take usually brings different reactions from each horse. But when one method doesn't work, I don't think of myself as a failure. I simply start using another technique.

Breaking and training a horse is hard work, but it's worth the effort. I know that I'll eventually have a great relationship with that horse as it carries me and walks alongside me through many different fields. But in the meantime, I've been bit, kicked, knocked down, snorted on, thrown off, pulled back, head butted, beat up, broken, worn out, pooped on, slammed against fences, walked on, stomped on, and run away from during the process of training. I often end up being dog tired with my clothes ripped and my blisters torn.

The horse is usually angry, hostile, obstinate, belligerent, unwilling, unteachable, stubborn, fighting, immovable, inflexible, and determined to remain a wild, selfish, self-gratifying, hay-eating, headstrong, and noncompliant equine. And I've learned through my years of breaking horses that the horse really thinks the problem is me and my interference in its life.

But eventually, even the horse learns that this isn't about me. It's about him. Knowing this, I keep the process going. Why? Because I really do love the horse even though the process is painful. I know where we're headed.

I sometimes wonder if the reason we see so much anger in young people is that we're not patiently preparing them for the world into which they are walking. Anger is an emotional response to not getting what you want. Young people tell me all the time that they're angry, but they don't know why. However, as I spend time with them and help them process what they feel and think, I sense that they just aren't ready to hit the world running, and their unpreparedness angers them.

Could this be one of the reasons young people headed off to college these days are so dependent on their parents? I'd be mad too if someone expected me to fulfill an expectation without preparing me for the task.

The point is this. We must prepare our children for the world in which they will live. As we raise our children, our emphasis must switch from protecting to preparing, from lecture to discussion, and from doing things for them to allowing them to learn to do things for themselves. Teens today are immature because we've created a teen world that lacks accountability and is short on responsibility. Parents must move young people from dependency on Mom and Dad to independence. It's a part of training. It's part of discipline. It allows and even motivates the maturing of relationships. And this shift will help young people "leave and cleave" when the time comes.

CHAPTER FIVE

THE PROBLEM OF PERFORMANCE-BASED RELATIONSHIPS

The next step on our journey in parenting teens is to deal with the issue of performance-based relationships. Parents must address this significant issue directly because most teens believe people will only love them up to a certain point. Beyond that point, whatever it is, the love is gone. As a result, they strive to do well and to work harder to never do wrong. Or they lose hope, give up, and rebel.

Their drive is rooted in a fear that if, by chance, they make a mistake or they do badly, they'll lose those they love. Unfortunately, their perception may contain a lot of truth. This fear is usually fostered in a child's younger years and is an extremely difficult pattern of thinking to break. It's a pattern that is developed from a belief that when they do something bad, they get in trouble, and when they do something good, they get rewarded.

The problem in Christian circles of young people is even worse. As a Christian kid, when you do something bad, you usually get eliminated. Leigh was no exception.

Leigh's Story

Leigh grew up with two loving parents who chose her to be in their family when they adopted her as a baby. I met her when she was 14, spinning out of control and letting everyone around her know she was unhappy. Her newfound role in life was to make everyone around her as miserable as possible.

She was setting fire to other kids' lockers in school, cussing out teachers, screaming at her parents, flunking every class she was taking, and acting like she was an uppity city girl who didn't care about anything or anyone. Her youth minister asked her to leave the youth group.

Her demise had come suddenly. Just a year earlier, she was the number one kid in the youth group. She loved school and always went to summer camp. But her youth minister's rejection put her over the top. I think it brought out feelings about being adopted that she had carried for years and that just now were coming to the surface. Feelings of rejection and abandonment. The better she performed in school and the better she acted in her relationships, the more confused she was about why her birth mother would give her up for adoption.

I immediately liked her.

Her parents, on the other hand, were devastated and exhausted. They had tried everything to make things work at home and had come to the conclusion that unless they got help outside the home, their spunky little ninth grader wasn't going to ever make it past her eleventh-grade year. I concurred.

I remember the first time I met her parents. Successful. Well-meaning. Sincere. And broken.

I felt as if I were at my first funeral as her dad shared their story and all they had done to help her. My eyes welled up with tears, and I felt as if my heart would break. I kept thinking this could have happened to our family.

I was torn. I was distraught. And I fell in love with the parents as much as I did the young lady who had come to live with us at Heartlight.

Leigh had a spunkiness about her. She was verbally interactive. She was a cute little girl who had traveled and who knew the ropes. And she knew how to get her way. I always thought that if we could get her a sales job somewhere, she could make us all millions. When she wasn't cussing me out, she was a pretty sweet girl.

I spent a year counseling with Leigh. We filled hours and hours of drinking coffee with laughter and crying as we talked about her adoption issues and her fear of not being able to live up to her parents' expectations. I tried to help her sort through her jumbled mess of emotions.

She completed our program and went home to a changed family. About two years later, the ugly serpent's head reappeared, and she wound up leaving home. We were all devastated to see her leave. Months later her mother called and asked if I would come to Kansas City and help find her and talk with her. I found a phone number, called her, and took her out to dinner. She ate two full entrees, and I knew her chosen lifestyle was tearing her apart. She was prostituting herself for drugs. She had lost her spunkiness and the gleam in her eye. She didn't laugh once. And neither could I. Seeing what she had become after I had spent so much time with her tore me apart. I could hardly imagine what her parents were going through.

Before I left, we stopped by a McDonalds, and I purchased $100 worth of gift certificates, not wanting to give her cash but wanting to put food in her belly.

She called me months later and asked if I could come see her. She was pregnant, didn't know whether to keep the baby, and said she finally wanted some changes. I flew to Kansas City the next morning and sat with a young lady who had not only been around the block a few times but had lived on its streets, eaten from its cans, and stood on its corners.

Leigh's story has been 20 years in the making. Putting such a long story into a few paragraphs is not easy. Leigh turned a corner when she realized her value was not determined by what she did, does, or will or will not do. She saw that she was valuable during her bad years and not just her good years.

Perception Is Truth to the One Who Perceives It

In performance-based relationships, people are valuable because of their actions, accomplishments, and achievements. They are accepted because they meet others' expectations. Take a moment and read those statements again because this understanding is critically important.

Performance-based relationships are conditional and convey or withhold love according to one's performance. This type of relationship holds the bar of expectation too high for most to attain and for almost anyone to maintain. When teens fail to meet others' expectations, they experience an overwhelming sense of disappointment, discouragement, despair, and despondency.

Most teens I have met with believe they have performance-based relationships with their parents. They believe their parents' love is conditional, based on how they behave.

You may not think this is true with your child, but perception is truth to the one who perceives it. And in all my years of working with struggling teens, I don't know of any young people who don't think their value is based on their performance. We parents would do well to show our kids that our love is not conditional and assure them that we do not want performance-based relationships.

Remember, what your child *thinks* is reality for him or her.

What Do You Communicate to Your Child?

What do you and your teen talk about? My guess is that you discuss such items as academics, work, behaviors, rules, privileges, sports involvement, picking the right friends, choosing the right clothes, cleaning up a room, performing chores, and obeying the rules of the house.

Now, take a moment and think about what else you talk about. Pretty short list? Get my point?

Most of what we talk about is performance oriented. This imbalance can create the impression that your relationship with your kids is determined by how they perform.

Mom and Dad, separating performance and relationship is critical. You want them to perform well, but their performance should have nothing to do with your relationship with them. They need to hear this repeatedly. If they don't understand this, their failures will eventually catch up with them and move them to frustration and futility. We parents must convey our love in ways that aren't based on performance. We need to help our kids understand that our love for them is totally unconditional, just as God loves us unconditionally.

Leigh thought her parents' love for her was based on her performance. Their successful lifestyle conveyed an unspoken demand for Leigh to perform for love. Her confusion wasn't her parents' fault. But parents are responsible to understand the way their lifestyle affects their child.

Leigh was already trying to perform. She believed her birth mother rejected her ("She gave me up, and she didn't even know me"), and now she was trying to prove her worth.

Every child wants to do well for his or her parents. "This one's for you, Mom." "Make your parents proud." "Don't embarrass your mom." "Win one for dear ol' Dad." "Do your best, Son."

But every mom and dad absolutely must release their children from living under the fear that the parents will take their love away if the children don't perform.

I am amazed at the negative comments some parents make to their kids. Those words stay with kids. I know because of what teens have shared with me over the years. Negative words, and sometimes just the absence of positive and affirming ones, can turn out the lights in a child's life. Imagine how kids feel when the most important people in their lives say things like these:

- "I'm ashamed of you."
- "You make me sick."
- "Get out of my sight."
- "I can't believe you."
- "Go to your room and away from me."
- "You're out of this youth group."
- "How could you do this to me?"
- "We should never have adopted you."

Comments like these set up kids for performance-based relationships and make them question their self-worth. They also drive kids to look elsewhere for their validation.

Don't think that words can't move a child to darkness. The myth that "sticks and stones can break my bones, but words will never hurt me" is a lie. I once heard someone say that the root of all mental illness is the fear that love is conditional. That might not be too far from the truth.

Expectations and Performance-Based Relationships

Do parents want good things for their kids? Absolutely. I'm not implying that you should abandon your high expectations for your children or that you shouldn't encourage them to be the best they can be. Just be careful not to communicate that your love is conditional, and make sure to assure them you'll always be there for them. I want my children (and now my grandchildren) to know that they can do nothing to make me love them less, and they can do nothing to make me love them more.

Parents must be careful how they communicate their expectations because every child will fail sometimes. And when your children don't perform well, they will think your relationship will suffer unless you convince them otherwise.

This is the critical juncture—and often the melting point—of a parent/child relationship. This is often when parents ask themselves how something so well-intentioned (their desire for their child to succeed) could work against them. And kids begin to think they could never live up to their parents' expectations—or God's.

Let me give you just one example.

Some popular programs motivate kids to save themselves sexually until marriage. And these programs are very well-intended. I'm sure many kids have committed themselves to abstinence and to save themselves sexually for the one they will someday commit their lives to. This is a well-founded expectation, based on biblical truth, agreed to by the teen, and rooted in nothing but a fine attempt to help teens live the way God desires for them to live.

But what happens to those promise makers who become promise breakers? What happens when you're no longer allowed in the club? What do kids think and feel when they make mistakes that eliminate them from something they have been striving for?

Of course, kids must experience the consequences of their choices. But sometimes we make those consequences worse than they need to be. We do well when we set high standards for kids to challenge them in activities that will help them be the best they can be. But we don't do well setting standards that exclude them should they make poor choices.

Spelling bees, softball, soccer, and video games are one thing. But when kids break a covenant they made with God, should they be thrown out of the club?

Why am I so concerned? One report has stated that 61 percent of those who make a pledge in one of these abstinence programs break their promise. And of those who don't break their promise not to have sexual intercourse, 55 percent engage in oral sex.

My point is not to trash any of these well-intended and effective programs. If they save just one person from sexual promiscuity, then they're worth every penny of expenditure. But kids need a plan B that doesn't eliminate them when they make poor choices. As I read Scripture, I find nothing that can eliminate us from God's family once we have come to know Him as Savior. Let's reflect that when we set our standards.

I conducted a Dealing with Struggling Teens seminar in Nashville and was amazed to hear the pastor of a 2800-member church tell me that the church currently didn't have a youth pastor—nor did very many kids attend the youth group.

When I walked into the room where we were holding the seminar, I noticed a set of standards displayed on the wall. The standards were certainly biblical—great expectations that were put there with the greatest of intentions. Each member of the youth group was to make these commitments:

- I will witness to everyone I meet.
- I will represent Christ in all I do.
- I will not sin and will strive to show Christ's love to everyone.
- I will devote my life to serving Him.
- I will live my life as an example of the One who died for me.
- I will never be selfish and will strive to think of others first.
- I will live my life as a sacrifice to Him who loves me and died for me.

I thought, *Man, these are some great expectations and standards.* I also thought, *No wonder kids don't want to be a part of this group!* No one could say anything bad about each of these biblical and well-meaning standards. But I knew I couldn't follow every one of them.

Dan Allender states this in his book *How Children Raise Parents*:

> We fail when certain standards of behavior, rather than grace and forgiveness, are assumed to be the core of Christianity…The result of a standards-oriented religion is the rise, if not the dominance, of a self-righteousness for those who appear to be doing what is expected. For those who aren't as adept at deceiving others, the outcome of a standards-driven Christianity will be shame.[1]

Our standards have not become too high for kids. But we eliminate our kids along the way when we don't provide for their continued engagement should they fail. Churches, pastors, youth pastors, and parents must be careful about setting up things that eliminate rather than finding ways to include people.

Grace is undeserved—it is available to those who have made poor choices. Forgiveness makes a way for us to include those who have fallen. If these two points were added to the wall of expectations, we wouldn't be losing millions of seventh graders from our youth groups by the time they reach the twelfth grade.

Changing a Performance-Based Relationship

People often ask me how we work with kids, why we are so successful in our approach, and why kids respond to us the way they do. The answer is simple. We love kids when they're at their worst.

I haven't met a teen yet who doesn't want to know he or she will continue to be loved when everything is a mess. You and I know loving is easy when all is going well. It's quite a different matter when everything is spinning out of control. So the first thing to do is to move toward your kids, especially if they are struggling and in a tough spot. Let them know you love them regardless. And if you don't love them, learn to. Tell them at least every week that you love them, not because of what they do but because of who they are.

Second, know that good relationships don't work well with lists, standards, and expectations. They work well with a love that says, "I love you, period." You may still get disappointed when you face disrespect, dishonesty, or disobedience. You may get frustrated when your child violates promises, acts inappropriately, or flunks a class. You may get mad when your child breaks something, makes mistakes, is deceitful, or lies to you. But you can still love her. And loving her doesn't take away consequences. It just means that you can separate her actions from the way you love and value her.

Leigh learned through the years that people could love her when she was a mess. My years with Young Life taught me to proclaim the gospel of Jesus Christ across a bridge of friendship and not to stop if kids don't respond. St. Francis of Assisi said, "At all times share the gospel, and when necessary, use words." My love for Leigh has nothing to do with what she's done, what she is doing today, or what she will do. I'm just thankful she knows she's loved.

I pray the same is true for your child.

CHAPTER SIX

WHY DOES MY CHILD ACT THIS WAY?

Parents who bring their out-of-control kids to Heartlight consistently ask, "Why does my child act this way?" They are distraught, exhausted, desperate for help, and trying to get a handle on their children's behavior. They want to stop the downward spiral of inappropriate habits and actions. Their question opens the door to even more questions:

- "Why has my child chosen this type of behavior?"
- "What is my child trying to accomplish?"
- "When did this inappropriate behavior begin?"
- "What is my child trying to say?"
- "What caused my child to move in this direction?"
- "What does my child really want?"
- "What message am I supposed to hear?"
- "What have I missed?"
- "Why am I having a hard time finding answers?"
- "Why does he act the way he does?"
- "When will this inappropriate behavior end?"

Sound familiar? I'm sure it does if your child is displaying mystifyingly new and inappropriate behavior.

Asking questions like these and seeking honest answers is a critical process. It will move you to make some changes in the way you run your home, in the way you parent your child, or in the way you offer alternatives and opportunities to your teen. Ashley and her parents provide us a great example.

Ashley's Story

When I first met Ashley, she was a ninth grader from upstate New York. As her parents were checking her into Heartlight, I asked if she wanted to take a walk around the property, see the houses and the horses, meet some of the other young people, and get a feel for the place she was going to spend her next nine months. I was really just looking for an opportunity for her to begin telling me what had been going on with her and her family.

As we walked and talked and had "our meet and greet" with other residents, they asked her, "What are you here for?" You would think she had just been convicted and was coming to Heartlight to serve her sentence!

Her answer was quick and compact. Without missing a beat, she would say, "I've been drinking and sleeping around, I've been depressed for a couple of years, I started cutting myself, and I can't stand my parents." The answer rolled off her tongue as if rehearsed and practiced.

I'm always amazed at how honest young people are about their own behavior. They are completely willing to share with their peers how screwed up they are (even if they are complete strangers). And remarkably, kids immediately bond in their dysfunction and pain. Birds of a feather do flock together.

Could your child be hanging out with kids who are rotten influences because they can identify with each other's hurts? Could your child be in as much pain as those other kids? I think so.

Perhaps these kids in all their mess are closer to community and connection than most adults, who have more of a tendency to hide and ignore their behavior and motives rather than express how they really feel. I sometimes wonder how people would respond if I was brutally honest when they ask me, "How you doin,' Mark?" I think I'd shock most people. Many would be uncomfortable with that much honesty. Deception is easier to handle than reality!

Despite some momentary awkwardness, people tend to communicate more deeply and even bond when they share a common hurt. Most churches and youth groups enjoy greater unity when honesty and truthfulness are laid on the table.

Because of Ashley's blunt and direct honesty, she immediately connected with her inquisitors and took her first step of deepening relationships with some future lifelong friends. And her honesty and frankness were an open invitation for me to ask some questions. So as we sat up at a horse barn, surrounded by saddles, lead ropes, and bridles, she began to "pony up" some answers.

The tears that filled her eyes were some of the biggest I'd ever seen as she tried to put answers to her feelings and purpose to her thoughts. She continued to open up, so I continued to ask questions.

She shared that her father was an alcoholic. She wept as she told me that her family had witnessed her dad's suicide. She painfully revealed that having a new stepdad was a constant reminder of all the things she could have had but lost because of her biological dad's death.

She went on to disclose that no one really knew her and that she didn't know why she was doing what she was doing—except to ease the pain of life. She said she felt confused, alone, lost, worn-out, exhausted, and hopeless. I wasn't surprised. She was describing how her mom and stepdad described the past two years of their lives.

I am surprised, though, to see how moved I am after 32 years of working with kids and their families. I'm amazed that a 14-year-old girl can bring me to tears. You'd think that after hearing thousands of tragic stories I wouldn't be fazed any more.

But even as I write Ashley's story, I tear up thinking about the pain she must have gone through. How life turned on a dime for her, how it changed so drastically in an instant. My heart breaks when I see the sins of a family passed on to their children. I ached to see people ignore the needs of this young lady, not because they didn't want to help but because they didn't know what her real needs were.

All I could say to Ashley as she shared her story was something like this: "Sweetheart, I don't blame you for what you've been doing. I can't imagine what you've been through. And if I were you, I might be drinking a little more. But your parents and I can't allow you to continue the path you're on because it will take you somewhere you don't want to be and perhaps even kill you."

She was quick to remind me that she didn't want to be at Heartlight either. I let out a laugh and told her I understood. I also shared with her that I was glad she didn't want to leave home and that she longed to return as soon as possible. I assured her that my job was to get her where she wanted to be.

Her behavior obviously wasn't the issue. Deeper issues were swirling around in Ashley's heart and head. We couldn't allow ourselves to be distracted by what we saw (her behavior); we needed to look deeper into her life and understand the motivation behind her behavior.

Behavior is never the issue. It always points to something bigger.

All Behavior Is Goal Oriented

If behavior is never the issue, then what is? Our task is to understand what prompts the behavior.

Before I go any further, I want to assure you that you cannot ignore your child's inappropriate behavior. You cannot justify its existence or allow destructive behavior to continue. But to stop your exploration into the real issues driving that behavior by focusing solely on the inappropriate behavior itself will keep you from experiencing true healing. You may stop the destructive behavior, but that alone will never reach the heart, where the real issues lie. And unless kids' hearts are changed, most of them will return to their old behavior when they go back to their old environment.

So how do you touch the heart of a troubled teen? Begin by understanding that behavior is always driven by a goal. This means you have to ask what the goal is. What do kids hope to accomplish through their actions?

- They want something.
- They want someone to hear their message.
- They want someone to take notice.
- They want to show their maturity and independence.
- They want to cover up the pain of an incident or trauma.
- They want to find acceptance.
- They want to know that they are more than the rejection they feel.
- They want relief.

Make no mistake—kids' behavior is driven by a goal. Unfortunately, struggling teens may not even know what that goal is! They may have no clue why they do what they do when they're doing it. And usually, the more bizarre the behavior, the more desperate the child is to find a remedy. A child's behavior then becomes an indicator of the depth of the issue she is seeking to resolve and of the lengths she is willing to go to in order to reach her goal.

Ashley's bizarre behavior was shouting to all that her struggle was much more than poor choices of behavior. Ashley was attempting to resolve her issues with her father's suicide, numb the pain of all she felt, and get some relief from the visual images stuck in her head. Those were her goals. And she chose the behaviors that were available to her.

The progression is pretty easy to understand but most difficult to decipher.

1. The behavior reflects the goals.
2. The goals represent a logical but perhaps unconscious plan to meet a need.
3. The need reflects the true intent of the behavior and actions.

When I say "needs," I mean those real or perceived conditions, possessions, environments, relationships, or actions that are essential or desired to fill an area where something is lacking or unattainable.

One of the reasons this seemingly simple system is actually quite complex is that an out-of-control teen's need are usually hard to sort out. And when you are able to accurately identify those needs, prioritizing them is always a challenge.

Neither Ashley nor her parents knew what her actual needs were. Her behavior was easy to understand. Who wouldn't be doing crazy things when people have done crazy things to them? But understanding a child's situation doesn't mean that one has to agree with the behavior. Nor does it give a child license to continue in the inappropriate behavior.

I commonly tell kids, "I understand where you're coming from." At times, they interpret that to mean I believe they are justified in what they're doing. I'm quick to remind them that I understand, but quicker to remind them that the behavior must stop. Ashley hated her mom and stepdad because they were keeping her from inappropriately coping with her issues. Sure, they were issues she hadn't picked, but she certainly had a choice in how to handle them.

We can easily understand why Ashley chose the behaviors she did. They were available to her. Drinking, cutting, and sleeping around became her coping mechanisms. And if anyone was going to get to the heart of her issues, they were going to have to look beyond the inappropriate coping mechanisms and determine what she really needed.

What Are the Needs?

Everyone has needs. The needs that a child has in middle school are far different from those needed in elementary school. Needs of a senior in high school are far different from a ninth grader's.

Needs are determined by several things. They can be created by losses in one's life (we'll talk about this more in the next chapter). They might be determined by tradition within a family or culture. The media can create needs in us we wouldn't have had otherwise. Our needs are often ingrained in us from values transferred from family and friends. Some needs—whether true or false—are passed on through generations.

One of the greatest needs I see in teens is the need for security. Security is a convinced awareness of being unconditionally and totally loved without needing to change in order to win that love. It is to enjoy a love freely given, which cannot be earned and therefore cannot be lost.

At the core of that security is the need we all have for relationships. It is built into us. Kids strive to have companionship where they will find validation, acceptance, value, honor, significance, meaning, and purpose.

Children are almost never able to articulate or even fully understand their needs, but they feel them intensely, and they choose behaviors that meet those needs. The behaviors they choose are accessible, possible, and (in their minds) effective.

When teens are caught in inappropriate behavior, I've found that they will stop and think when I ask, "Is it working for you?" Helping teens think about their situation and arrive at an understanding is far better than telling them what they must believe. This understanding about themselves will impact them more if they make conclusions about their behavior in response to your questions than if you give a lecture. Let them deduce what they need to. Let them come to the conclusions about their behavior. Kids are more capable of understanding their behavior than you might think.

When Behavior Changes

I rarely hear kids say, "You know, my mom just wasn't there for me during my teen years." Most of the time, teens think that their moms are there too much, always telling them what to do, encouraging when they need to, nagging when they have to.

Moms are just there. It's in their being. Every child knows it.

A child's relationship with his or her mom is like none other. Most kids feel that their moms will never leave them. The connection is very special. Because most young people perceive this relationship with their moms to be so secure and so deep, they feel more comfortable sharing deeper issues with Mom than with Dad. They also feel they can express their anger (sometimes very inappropriately) to Mom because moms just don't leave.

Dads, on the other hand, are thought to be cool if they hang out with their kids because that is not something they tend to do. Dads can more easily make themselves absent or even walk away. As a result, when kids become teens, they may not feel connected to their dads. This is especially true if the dad feels inadequate or incompetent. The result is that Dad can feel hurt when he senses a child moving away from him, or he can feel unneeded when there is the shift of relationship away from parents to peers.

When dads retreat or remove themselves from their children (or are removed from their children by divorce, death, or some other decision), problems will usually follow. Why? Because moms are the ones who instill a sense of value, and dads are the ones who validate it. All children need their fathers' "stamp of approval." When Dad's stamp of approval is not there, the child will look for validation somewhere else.

This is especially true of teenage girls. They need Dad to meet that need for validation—something only he can really fulfill. And with 12- to 14-year-old girls, this need is greater than ever. But sadly, dads often move away from their daughters at this time.

Kelley's Story

So what does a girl do when Dad isn't around? Some do what Kelley did. When asked about her relationship with her dad, Kelley told me what I've heard a thousand times. "My dad wasn't there when I needed him most." Cop-out? Excuse? Justification for inappropriate behavior? No.

But Kelley's response is not unique. If I only heard this from a few girls through the years, that would be one thing. The fact that I've heard it a thousand times over the years means this must be a critical issue.

Let's look at Kelley's story to see what we can learn. As we do, I want you to pay special attention to this young girl's heart. You will see the goal that was really driving Kelley's behavior.

Like any girl, Kelley needed her dad during her early teen years. She needed affirmation, validation, direction, protection, encouragement during difficult times, honor, priority, and participation.

And for years she had gotten these from her dad. He coached softball. He took her on trips with him. He left work early to spend time with her. They went to father-daughter retreats. They had a date night. They would buy each other matching pajamas for Christmas. Tickle fights. School projects. Special gifts for her from his business trips. She would draw pictures and cut out designs for him to put on his office door.

Kelley and her dad were as close as any dad and daughter could be. In fact, they were so tight that they felt a sense of loss anytime they were not together. Something is very special about the father-daughter relationship in the elementary school years, and Kelley and her dad had one very special relationship.

During your kids' elementary years, you transfer value to them by what *you allow them to do with you.* In their junior high years, you help them feel valuable by what *you do with them.* In their high school years, you communicate value *by what you provide.*

As Kelley moved into her junior high years, she felt that Dad moved away from her. Not great timing because these are the years when other girls are cruel and hateful. It's a time of awkwardness. It's a time of change. It's a time of puberty, emotions, tears, periods, bras, and new perspectives.

It's a time when the exposure to life outside the confines of the home begins. And of course, hormone-laden boys enter the picture. For many girls, this is when they need their dads the most, but their dads are present the least.

Some have called these years the wonder years. This is true for some parents—they wonder why they ever had kids! Other parents wonder if they should be on Valium during their child's junior high years or if they should just use duct tape and lock their kids up during this time!

There's no doubt that the seventh and eighth grades are tough times for youngsters. And this is when kids begin to act out and start riding an emotional roller coaster.

Some people may believe children are shaped most by their elementary years or by their high school years, but I believe these early teenage years are the most important.

Personally, the things that happened in my seventh- and eighth-grade years have left a mark on me. Getting beat up, moving to a new home, and realizing I had a big nose, I had chicken legs, and I wasn't as smart as I thought I was are all vivid memories. Ridicule, sarcasm, awkwardness, and change are all a part of the seventh- and eighth-grade package.

If Dad isn't there during this time of great need, he is setting the stage for disaster. Kids' needs don't go away. They remain the same. Kids will just find different ways to meet them.

Maybe Kelley's dad began to disappear because the sports he used to coach—where he connected with his daughter—were being coached by someone at the junior high. Or maybe he had a hard time making the transition from being a dad to a little girl to being a dad to a young lady. Then again, perhaps his occupation required him to work more, and time became a scarcity. Or perhaps Dad didn't change his style of parenting and move from the concrete thinking of a young child to the abstract thinking of a growing woman.

Maybe Dad had cancer treatments and he couldn't be there like he used to be. Maybe he started playing golf and devoted more time to his clubs than his daughter. Maybe he decided to go back to school. Maybe Dad decided to finally deal with his alcoholism. Maybe he had an affair. Maybe he died. Maybe a divorce separated this young lady from her dad. Maybe his parents got sick, and he had to spend all his time caring for their needs.

Kelley's dad could have disappeared for a number of reasons. Some understandable, some not. But whatever the reason, he wasn't there for her.

So now someone else would meet Kelley's needs. And now she

had the additional feelings of rejection, abandonment, lack of male companionship, and a loss of worthiness. She no longer felt valued.

So the allure of a new relationship with a young man pulled her. She began to look for someone who would feel the same as her, who would understand, who would make her feel important, and who would come alongside her in her struggle to fill the void left by an absent dad.

Her needs remained the same. Her goal was to meet those needs. Her behavior changed to reach that goal.

Kelley began to hang out with a new group of kids, especially one young man who she stated, "is a lot like my dad." As her friendship grew with this 15-year-old kid, so did their physical relationship. And at 15, Kelley became pregnant.

She was the star cheerleader at her school, and her friends gathered around her and adopted her as their new project. She became a novelty, a pregnant glamour girl whom everyone adored. Youth ministers invited her to come talk to their youth group about the evils of a sexual relationship.

But inside, Kelley was struggling. Struggling so much that she began to smoke pot.

I've found that most people who smoke dope are trying to combat their own depression…an observation based on 30 years of spending time with kids who smoke pot. It's one of the hardest things to break kids of, one of the most damaging drugs with long-term consequences on the high school landscape.

And on the nights when Kelley wasn't smoking, she was drinking. And she was still sexually active. Kelley was a young girl in deep pain. Unbelievably, most people thought she had it all together. But in reality, she was a mess. And her actions weren't working for her.

She gave birth to a little girl that Kelley's parents decided to raise while Kelley secretly continued her external habits to combat her internal confusion. One day she was arrested with enough dope to choke a horse. All of a sudden, Kelley's hidden actions were exposed, and her world came crashing down around her.

The community that supported her as she wrestled through her plight began to reject and shun the one they had embraced. The emotional roller coaster became much too hard for Kelley to bear, and the young girl who was once the pride of the town was now a pathetic mess of a teen who really just wanted to have her dad around.

I wonder sometimes if the reason dads get so mad at the young men who steal their daughters is that they are reminded of what they haven't done. They see how they have failed with their daughters.

What If You Can't Determine the Needs?

Most parents would say they understand the model I have described and agree that all behavior is driven by some goal. And they would look at Ashley's and Kelley's bizarre behavior and would agree that these two young ladies had reasons for their actions. They would probably even agree with me that they should be messed up.

But then they would add, "But what about my child? We can't see any losses, can't determine what the needs are, and can't put a finger on the real issues!"

Unfortunately, sometimes a child's behavior defies explanation. I have seen situations where no cause-and-effect equation or logical pattern or identified loss is evident. Sometimes behavior can't be categorized as rebellion and isn't caused by immaturity.

In these situations, time will usually expose the motives and goals behind the behavior. All you can do in these instances is to make every effort to keep further inappropriate behavior from happening with the hope that one day your child will begin to process what he or she is doing and come to some conclusions.

But even when we can't explain kids' behavior, my encouragement to all parents is not to disengage from their children when those kids might need them the most. If parents abandon children during a time of difficulty or bad behavior, who will help them process the way they think about who they are during a time of struggle? In difficult times, parents and children both tend to withdraw. Kids' withdrawal is based on shame and guilt. Your withdrawal may be because of the pain their behavior is causing. Or perhaps you disengage because you don't understand what is going on. But if you pull out emotionally during this time, how will your kids ever learn about God's grace, His acceptance, or His love when they don't feel too lovely? Remember J.R.R. Tolkien's statement, "Faithless is he that says farewell when the road darkens."[1]

Is My Child Wired Differently?

Some kids' behavior can only be explained by the fact that they are just wired differently. These kids have had no particular crisis or trauma that would move them toward such behavior. Nor do they have some remarkable need that a parent would notice. It's just the way they behave.

I divide these young people into two groups. The first are those who might have what I call silent issues. These issues are usually invisible until they are reflected in kids' screaming behavior...behavior that many times is misdiagnosed as being rebellious, obstinate, belligerent, selfish, stubborn, or strong willed.

The correct diagnosis might be attention deficit disorder, personality disorders, obsessive compulsive disorder, logic sequence problems, intelligence or emotional challenges, or learning disabilities. I'm not a psychiatrist or a psychologist and can't diagnose these things, but I have been around young people who have these behavior issues and am amazed at how often these kids are misdiagnosed. I can only imagine where a child would be if the real problems were diagnosed accurately at a much earlier stage.

Dan came to us as a 17-year-old and was flunking out of school. He was relating to people inappropriately, using drugs, sneaking away from home at night, and doing anything he could to ignore his parents' wishes.

After Dan arrived at Heartlight, we saw that he actually wanted to think before he acted, but he couldn't. He wanted to get help in counseling, but he just couldn't connect the dots. And he wanted to be socially acceptable, but he just couldn't make it happen.

As time passed, we found that Dan had a second-grade reading level, a very low IQ, learning disabilities, and a logic sequence problem.

For whatever reason, Dan's parents and teachers had never seen these problems and had interpreted his behavior as an attitude problem coupled with rebellion and anger. They didn't know. And the effects of not knowing caused amazing damage.

Dan's parents had to adjust their hopes for their child. He wasn't going to be a brain surgeon. He wasn't going to go to college. He would need to choose an occupation where he could use his hands. Their response to his inadequacies began to change when they realized that they misunderstood his issues.

By the way, I've found that some families don't want to accept who their child is or recognize that their child's future is not going to be what they thought it was going to be. Dan's parents wanted desperately for Dan's problems to be rebellion, apathetic attitudes, and anger (because those things can change), but their eventual acceptance of their son's true issues did change Dan's behavior. The pressure was off, and they lowered their expectations to an acceptable and achievable level.

Dan was no longer frustrated for not being where everyone else seemed to think he needed to be. He was no longer angry for not getting what he wanted. What he thought he wanted was really what everyone else wanted for him…something he could never achieve.

And finally, Dan's rebellion ceased. When Dan and his parents accepted his issues, he began to live as a real person, not some virtual person who was never going to live up to the fantasy placed on him by his parents. They realized he was acting inappropriately because he couldn't fulfill his parents' expectations.

Other Idiosyncrasies

The second group of young people that are wired differently are those who are born with either a low self-image, a need for thrills or excitement, a love for creativity, or other unique tendencies. They are that way because they're made that way, and chances are they will always be that way. You can try all you want, but these kids won't change because they can't.

In these cases, parents need to learn to appreciate the uniqueness of their children. They must find the treasure in their children's hearts and rejoice in the way God created them.

Curious vs. Goal-Oriented Behavior

The Internet is a fairly new and useful tool. What it offers to us all is amazing. But what it exposes our children to can be so damaging.

I'm not talking about sexualized sites and pornography. I'm talking about exposure to some things that are just bizarre and corruptive. A bad combination of availability and curiosity can sometimes have deadly results.

A few years ago I had never heard of cutting, a form of self-injury. I had never heard of the choking game, also called space monkey, where people choke themselves, depriving their brain of oxygen momentarily to achieve a euphoric druglike high. I didn't know that anorexia would become the new diet. Or that "huffing" certain inhalants around the house would allow kids to get high and overcome their boredom.

Young people are curious. And through the Internet they are encouraged to experiment out of intrigue and fascination. Because it's available, and because kids hear about it, they try it.

They may have a reason behind their behavior, but they most likely don't have a reason at all. It's not about sex, drugs, or alcohol. These are just alternative ways of being deviant and curious without committing other sins.

Will there be new temptations in the future? Absolutely. Will they entice our kids to wrong behavior? You bet. And the motive behind the behavior? To quote President Clinton, "I did it, because I could."[2]

Normal but Inappropriate Behavior

A man recently told me that his son has a problem with pornography. As we talked, he stated that his son came to him feeling guilty because he had been on the Internet and seen some things that were inappropriate.

Is viewing pornography inappropriate? Yes. Did the son have a problem with pornography? Perhaps not. It may just have been an issue of availability.

A woman is one of God's most beautiful creations. God created man with a desire to enjoy a woman's beauty. A man's longing for a woman is normal.

But fulfilling that longing outside of marriage is inappropriate. Period. And so is indulging in fantasies with graphic images. Just as much as I believe that nothing good happens after midnight, I also believe that guys shouldn't have computers in their bedrooms. It's too much of a temptation.

So when you see this type of behavior, it may simply be an availability issue. Solve the availability problem, and the behavior will take care of itself.

So Now What?

As we have seen, behaviors can spring from various causes. Regardless of the reason for inappropriate behavior, any child can learn to be obedient, respectful, and honest. And all kids can learn to not do things just as easily as they learned to do them. Understanding the source of your child's behaviors helps you choose the right approach for tackling those behaviors.

In any of these issues, immaturity calls for boundaries, rebellion calls for consequences, and some behaviors call for restrictions.

Remember, most behavior has a motive or at least a reason. Those motives and reasons should be the focus of your correction. The behavior is not the issue. It may be the presenting problem and need to be corrected, but wise parents look also to the cause for the behavior. They help children learn that inappropriate behavior is not getting them to the place they want to be.

Look deeper with the eyes of your heart so see what is behind your child's behavior. Your child may not say it, but he will appreciate your effort to find the root of the problem and help him change his life.

CHAPTER SEVEN

THE IMPORTANCE OF PAIN

I rushed to the airport, determined to get settled in plenty of time to start writing this chapter. I had planned my trip home so I could have the full day to work on it. I even saved a couple of hundred dollars by purchasing a ticket that would allow another stop, another plane, and an extra four hours of travel so I would have plenty of time to write.

As I went through airport security, I followed the usual routine of pulling off my belt, taking off my watch, pulling out my computer, and taking off my shoes. I placed everything on the conveyer belt to have them X-rayed. As I was standing in the line, the lady behind me was doing the same thing. But when she pulled out her laptop, it fell out of her hands and headed to the floor.

About that time everything started to go into slow motion. As I watched in disbelief I realized—much too late—that the computer was headed straight for my foot. And before I could react it nailed my big toe, right at the base of my toenail.

When it hit, I felt as if someone had just cut my toe off. The pain raced to my head. I broke out in a sweat, and I kicked her computer like a hockey puck across the floor. Thoughts of anger and waves of pain overwhelmed me, and I started feeling faint.

I hobbled to a seat with all my stuff and pulled off my sock to find that my toenail had already pulled away from my toe. And the pressure underneath the nail just continued to build. The redness looked like someone had just hammered my toe. She had.

I thought I could walk it off and put it out of my mind. Instead, the pain increased. I still ordered my latte—sweating and just looking for some relief, I took a sip, but the pain was so great, it didn't taste right. So I threw it away and hobbled to my gate, barely able to think about anything but the pain shooting through my foot.

I got on the plane, and as we took off, I sat praying for a miracle, hoping for relief, and trying not to swear. The pain just got worse. I could barely sit still. *How can a toe hurt so much?*

By the time I finally arrived in Dallas, the triple dose of Advil was beginning to work. And by the time I got home—some nine hours after I left Chicago—my toe was still uncomfortable, but it was tolerable.

The Power of Pain

I was amazed where the pain had taken me. It impacted every part of my life. It changed my attitude. I was short with people, and the day became very, very long.

Things that should have been funny weren't. I was angry instead of happy. Because I was experiencing such severe pain, I couldn't stay focused. I was jumpy. I was hyper. From the moment the pain hit nothing was enjoyable. The food didn't taste good, the coffee tasted worse, and my appetite for anything normal was replaced by a gut ache. Important calls, schedules, and conversations were no longer foremost on my mind. The only thing that became important was relief for my pain. It became my focus, my purpose, and my sole desire.

What Pain Produces

We've all endured times of intense pain. Perhaps you are there right now. Or maybe someone around you—perhaps your child—is showing the same symptoms I had.

Pain usually produces the same response in all of us. What was once important becomes irrelevant. The pain itself overwhelms every part of life, and we are focused on finding relief. My own pain produced some things in me that are not part of my normal makeup. For instance, my pain made me more sensitive to others. I noticed hurting people more than I had noticed them before. People with hurt feet, on crutches, in wheelchairs, limping. I also slowed down. And I started to ask for help (something that I don't usually do).

My pain also taught me a few things. First, it taught me to watch out for flying laptops. Second, I learned to keep my shoes on as long as I could. Third, I'm more careful to make sure I don't injure someone else as I had been injured. But most of all, I learned that most people operate in pain. And maybe some of their behavior is a result of the pain that they're experiencing.

Embracing Pain

I am amazed that when we are in pain, we think the pain is going to last forever. Yet most pain in our lives is temporary.

Remember 2 Corinthians 4:17? It reminds us that pain is not only temporary but also has an incredible outcome: "For our light and momentary troubles are achieving for us an eternal glory that far outweighs them all" (NIV).

So, what if you never face this kind of pain in your life? Will you never learn important lessons or achieve an eternal glory? And what if you try to protect your child so he or she never experiences pain? Might you both miss out on some important life lessons?

C.S. Lewis states, "God whispers to us in our pleasures, speaks in our conscience, but shouts in our pains: It is His megaphone to rouse a deaf world."[1] Pain is an instrument He uses to expose who we really are and how life really is, and to bring us to a place in life where we will seek Him for answers. We all desire to run from pain, but it is in fact a tool that causes us to question our current circumstances and reevaluate our goals and motives.

To avoid pain in your own life—or the life of your child—allows childish thinking and foolish behavior to continue. And it results in greater pain.

I don't know of any parents who enjoy watching their children go through painful times. Everything in us wants to bail our children out of their pain and keep them from hurting. But God continues to show me that pain is an instrument He uses—and perhaps at times even causes—to motivate us to move to a new level of personal and spiritual maturity.

The Value of Pain

I have learned that God uses pain to develop sensitivity in us and to help us grow. I realize now that by trying to avoid pain, I have sometimes gotten in the way of God's plan, preventing Him from molding me and the people I love into the people that He desires us to be. As hard as it is to admit, my well-intentioned actions, at times, have precluded God's work in people's lives.

I have learned that our attempt to lessen our children's pain only postpones the inevitable. And when we do, the suffering comes back at a later date when the consequences of choices are greater. Let me give you an example.

I've always been a supporter of homeschooling. I still am. For all the good reasons, I think it is truly a great idea. So don't read into this example that I am against homeschooling. But I do have some concerns about how through homeschooling we can overprotect our children and not allow them to develop critical decision-making skills that will help them later in life.

Homeschooling does protect. That's not a problem. But, in some instances, homeschooling does not allow kids to be exposed (a little bit at a time) to a world that is bent on their destruction. Parents become overly protective because they know the hardships that kids face. They don't want to allow their kids to experience pain.

As a result, children grow up in a painless environment and aren't forced to develop their decision-making skills. By being exposed to difficult and potentially painful situations, kids learn how to share, how to handle conflict, how to make choices, how to walk away from dangerous situations, how to operate in social settings, how to fit in, how to function as maturing adults, and how to behave appropriately when everything around them is inappropriate.

As parents, you and I certainly want to protect our children. But we must also *prepare* our children. And by precluding pain, or not allowing our children to hurt, we let them live in a bubble that can carry them to their destruction. Our well-intended insulation and isolation of our children can bring about unintended devastating results.

Allowing a child to experience pain is difficult. For example, the same sympathetic heart that moves a parent to adopt a child can keep the child from experiencing pain. The same generosity that drives you to provide for your child can keep your child from learning how to live without some things. Your desire to protect can prevent your child from struggling through the process of discovery.

We parents must see that this momentary pain motivates our children to reconsider options, reflect on choices, and reevaluate where their current choices have placed them.

A child will only touch a hot stove once. But kids today aren't even allowed to touch that hot stove. Matter of fact, many aren't even allowed around the stove because Mom's doing all the cookin'. She is controlling things, and controlling them tightly.

But that kind of control and overprotection is detrimental to a child's development. Mom, Dad, understand that experience is a good teacher. And allowing a child to fail is sometimes a good thing. Permitting a child to feel hurt and the pain associated with that hurt can do some pretty good things for that child.

You know, I think I'd brush and floss my teeth a whole lot more if my dentist didn't use Novocain to deaden the pain of drilling when she fills my cavities. I would do what I needed to do to avoid that pain. Pain is a powerful motivator.

Can Sitting in Jail Be a Good Thing?

A few years ago, a father named Bill called me on Christmas Eve and asked for a few minutes of my time. I could tell he was desperate, angry, and hurting just by the trembling of his voice.

After a few well-wishing statements, he began to tell me that his son, Brian, had just been arrested for possession of narcotics, for resisting arrest, and for driving under the influence. Now he was sitting in a jail cell in Seattle.

Bill explained that the family was supposed to go to Colorado the next day for a skiing vacation with the extended family. It was their vacation of a lifetime, one they had planned for a long time and had anticipated for months.

Bill told me that he could bail out his son, and the son could join the family on the trip, but Bill was having second thoughts about rescuing his son. He didn't know what would be best.

Was it better to bail his son out of jail and take him on the trip (after all, it was Christmas) or leave him to spend the next ten days in jail while the family was off enjoying their time together on this long-awaited vacation? He didn't know whether he should endure the pain of not having his son on the trip—and the possibility of messing up a family vacation—or whether he should allow his son to experience the pain of his choices. Tough decision.

Brian, Bill's son, had been raised in a home where he was given everything, had to work for little, and was pretty much enabled to do just about anything he wanted to do. I knew from previous conversations that his dad was always bailing him out of things and that Brian never had to pay the price for anything. He was always being rescued.

Call it what you want, but this young man had been enabled, permitted, and allowed to continue in his foolish thinking and crazy behavior, never touching the hot stove of life. He had never experienced the pain that would correct his thinking and steer him toward good choices.

So I told Bill to let him sit. I encouraged him to see that now was the time for him to stop rescuing his son and allow Brian to pay the price for his poor and immature choices. It would be a lesson that Brian would not forget, and one that would not come easy. But it was time. And taking a stand now might save Brian's life in the long run.

Quite honestly, I didn't think Bill would take my suggestion or even listen to my advice. But when I called Bill in Colorado a few days later and asked him how things were going on their vacation, he tearfully said it was miserable. It was so hard to think that his son was back home in a jail cell when they were supposed to be enjoying their family time together. But he went on to say that he knew the decision to have Brian sit tight was the right one.

Personally, I think the whole process was really more about Bill than Brian. And frankly, the whole family was elated that Dad had finally stood up to his son and wasn't going to participate in his son's antics any more. He had come to realize he was empowering his son to live a life that could eventually lead to his death.

As hard as it was for Brian's dad to leave him in that jail cell, and as tough as it was for Brian to stay there, it ended up being one of the greatest weeks in Brian's life. That week everything came crashing down. For the first time Brian knew a brokenness. And for someone who had always had it all together, the experience was profound.

In his brokenness he made a commitment to Christ—a commitment that was rooted in a deep understanding of his need for a Savior. In fact, after Brian was released from jail, he commemorated his transformation with a tattoo across the underside of his arm, where these beautiful words appear: "He who has the Son has life, he who does not have the Son of God does not have life."

Brian's dad had finally allowed pain to have its full effect on his son. And Brian's life was transformed. The only thing I wonder is whether Brian would have gotten there sooner if his dad hadn't bailed him out so much. Who knows?

As I have thought about Brian's story, Proverbs 19:18 (NIV) comes to mind: "Discipline your son for in that there is hope; do not be a willing party to his death."

I believe God is encouraging us as parents to allow pain in our children's lives to help set the boundaries of choices, and to let consequences have their full impact in order to help our children heed the warnings: Don't go there.

Rescuing Can Make Things Worse

Parents are wired to protect their children. It's natural. But parents are also wired to prepare their children. Unfortunately, our generation focuses more on protection than it does preparation, which is why many teens today are so immature.

They don't grow up because we don't let them. Even though most teens are capable of being adults intellectually and biologically, our well-intended actions can shelter, confine, control, and anesthetize our children from the hardships that are actually vital to their growth. Our actions or restrictions and limits don't prepare, they hinder.

Let me give you some scenarios I believe can inhibit you from preparing your child for his or her future. These are scenarios I have seen played out over and over again and normally end up hurting a child instead of helping.

- Parents ignore the low performance of their children. They constantly complain about teachers. They are reluctant to accept the fact that their children may have a low IQ or an academic problem.

- Mom and Dad keep rescuing their son every time he gets into trouble at school, saying that he's just "all boy." As a result, they postpone their son's acceptance of consequences for inappropriate behavior by allowing his childish behavior to continue far too long.

- Dad fears confronting a daughter who treats her mother terribly. He thinks if he demands respect in his home, she'll run away. She ends up ruining all her relationships with family members and leaves anyway.

- Parents are afraid to set rules and boundaries within their home. They know that the children won't like the new policies, and they want to avoid difficult conversations.

- A father bails his child out of speeding tickets and personally pays the insurance rate hikes. Rather than grounding the son from using the car, he empowers him to continue his reckless behavior, and the son finally kills someone.

- Parents don't let their children handle their own money, fearing they might bounce a check or misuse the funds. So kids never learn how to handle finances, and when they get married, the marriage falls apart because of financial mismanagement.

- Mom is afraid to follow through on the consequences of her kids' behavior. She's never been strong and is not confident in that role.

- A mom bails a child out of jail because she doesn't want her daughter to be around the inmates. The pain of thinking that her child is in jail or detention for a night prevents her from allowing the daughter to experience the pain that is necessary to stop the type of behavior that got her there. (By the way, your child will probably learn the lesson the first time something like this happens if you remain strong, and she will ultimately bless you for doing what was needed at such a critical time.)

- Parents are afraid to accept the fact that their children are spinning out of control for fear they might look bad in the community. (Most kids eventually nosedive in such a case, and the whole community is keenly aware of the failure.)

- Mom and Dad never say no.

- Parents don't get help for children who struggle socially until the children's relationships are so bad they are damaged.

- Mom just can't believe that her son would "ever do such a thing," so she sweeps his behavior under the rug, only to have it crawl back into the light when the local police knock on the front door.

- Parents won't stand up for what they believe for fear of their son's response. They wonder why their child doesn't stand up for what he believes with his friends.

Many times, parents' fear prevents them from walking with their children through difficult times or times of pain. When a teen makes a pretty serious blunder, parents should never ignore the situation. Two wrongs never make a right. When children are wrong, parents need to do what's right.

Facing the Pain

Pain will come as children mature and start to take on their own identity. Watching children mature can be painful. They will make bad choices as they strive for independence. But this is critical if they are to be prepared for healthy adulthood. It is a part of growing up. And for the most part, parents haven't done a very good job of allowing kids to experience and learn from mistakes as they continue to protect their teens as they did when the children were young.

Let me give you a good example. I'm all for every kid on the team getting a trophy when they're in the first few grades of their elementary years. But to give trophies to the whole team in eighth grade when they didn't win is not helping those kids prepare for what is about to hit them as they enter high school.

Why do we do that? I think we have two reasons. First, we don't want our children to be ignored or rejected. We don't want our children to experience that pain.

But I think we have another reason: Sometimes it's more about us than it is about our kids. Because we as parents can't deal with our own pain, our kids pay the price and won't grow up prepared to handle what they will be forced to face one day.

So we need to be prepared as parents to allow our kids to go through pain. And pain will come in many forms.

Pain will come when you begin to have difficult conversations with your daughter about values. You hurt when you realize she is not on the same page as you in moral and ethical areas. She needs you most during these painful discussions. And if you disengage from her during this time, who is going to help her formulate those values?

Pain will come when you confront foolish thinking—yours or your child's. No parents like to have their foolish ways or thinking exposed.

And no kids like having their foolish thinking uncovered. But that doesn't mean you don't do it. Lovingly confront your children, and be open to their criticism of you.

Pain will come when you and your son have conflicting ideas, when you don't agree on his relationships, when you expose his motives, or when he exposes yours.

Pain will come when you confront your kids regarding behaviors that are out of line or just wrong. These discussions may get a little heated. If you can't stand the heat, I encourage you to turn down the temperature a little bit. Take a small break, and then get back together to discuss things further.

By the way, I'm amazed at how fearful most parents are about anger and the expression of it. Scripture assures us that we can be angry and not sin. Anger can in fact be good. The intensity of our anger can reflect the longings of our heart for something good in the lives of our kids.

Pain will come when parents function as goalkeepers. The goalkeeper is the one who has to constantly point toward a goal and say, "Yes, this is the way we're headed," or "No, this is not the way we're going." Both those statements can be painful.

Pain will come when your daughter begins her quest for independence. Let me encourage you not to confuse this desire for independence with selfishness. You want your daughter to be independent when she leaves home and goes off to school or work. But independence comes at a price.

None of us enjoy these times, but they are opportunities to guide and steer your child through rough waters when the guidance and steering are needed the most. Don't bail out when the going gets rough.

Dads and Pain

Avoiding pain is easy, especially for us dads. We are great at checking out.

I see dad after dad who boils, stews, and allows unresolved issues to destroy his relationship with his child. Or who avoids conflict by compromising his standards.

Then there are those who cover up problems by overindulging their kids...creating a deflection from the problem and causing even more problems.

Dads, we can choose to ignore what's really happening with our children and steer clear of the painful experience of dealing with the issues. But by ignoring or avoiding situations that cause pain, you miss incredible opportunities to move your child *through* the pain. And moving through the pain produces character that can't be developed any other way. So when you sidestep painful situations in your child's life, you are only allowing his or her immaturity and foolish and wrong thinking to continue.

Dads, don't put it off. Don't wait until you feel like the moment is right—it will never feel right. Do what is right, regardless of your feelings.

The Other Side of Pain

Pain has an amazing way of bringing about maturity. The young people who come to live with us in our residential program at Heartlight are often very mature. They are young men and women who have been forced to struggle through difficult and painful issues of death, divorce, victimization, and hurt. That doesn't mean they don't have issues they have yet to resolve. But they do have a maturity about them because of the pain they are experiencing.

For example, kids in pain often find a new sensitivity to others who are hurting. They are able to make connections with those who are in pain. They feel.

I'm amazed that even though my generation has been so bent on relationships, we have been afraid of conflict. We seem to think conflict was never meant to be a part of relationships. And because we have avoided conflict in our relationships, we now have to develop programs of connecting—small groups, accountability groups, group therapy, and community groups—in order to accomplish what would have been achieved had we understood that conflict is a core part of relationships.

The path God has provided for you and your child to connect may be the very path you have been trying to avoid.

Growing Your Child Through Pain

Parents who understand the value of pain and conflict begin to see struggles in a new light. They begin to understand that their children are seeking answers in life, so the parents embrace the pain and struggles as opportunities to move their children to a deeper understanding about their true need for a Savior. They don't provide all the answers to their children's searching; they provide direction.

If parents always give their searching children the answers rather than allowing them space to work through their questions, the children will lose their motivation to continue seeking. On the other hand, when parents remain engaged and give direction without always giving answers, they encourage their kids to keep searching. And when a child begins to seek on his own, he finds.

Pain and discomfort motivate. In fact, your teens will continue in their behavior until the pain that is a result of the behavior is greater than the pleasure derived from it.

Of course, we shouldn't cause pain in our children's lives. But an appropriate level of discomfort will help our children move away from a place they don't want to be. The key for parents is to remain engaged when their children go through pain. Be available to give some good guidance and clear options.

Kids in Pain

Young people in pain don't always make good decisions. Shoot, they don't make good decisions when they aren't in pain! So you need to be understanding and find out what is bothering them. As you do, you will begin to move toward your child when she is in pain. She needs you to walk with her through difficult times.

By the way, young people in pain will sometimes appear to be more selfish than those who are not. Even when they experience grace, they may not accept it as such. They are so set on self-preservation that they often wouldn't be able to see grace if it bit them on their nose!

Remember that often when teens are acting out, they are just trying to get out of their pain. Their choices are usually designed to help them find relief from their pain.

Pain causes people to do things that they wouldn't normally do. And wise parents need to be there to help guide their kids even when times are ugly. Remember, God is at work in their lives, and we don't want to be an impediment to His process.

Please hear me on this: Pain never justifies a person's inappropriate behavior. But an understanding of your child's pain helps you know how to help. Yes, you must hold the line. But sometimes a tight grip hurts, and other times a firm grip gives your child a sense of security.

So when your child begins to act inappropriately, you might want to stand back, evaluate, give it some time (perhaps 24 hours), and then determine what to do. Decide whether the pain your child is going through is enough to teach him or her the lesson that's needed. Often times it is.

Concluding Thoughts

As we end this chapter, I would like to leave you with some powerful Scriptures to think about. These verses are found in Romans 8 (NIV), and they can encourage and strengthen your heart as you seek to parent your child through his or her pain.

- For you did not receive a spirit that makes you a slave again to fear (verse 15).

- Now if we are children, then we are heirs—heirs of God and co-heirs with Christ, if indeed we share in his sufferings in order that we may also share in his glory (verse 17).

- I consider that our present sufferings are not worth comparing with the glory that will be revealed in us (verse 18).

- But if we hope for what we do not yet have, we wait for it patiently (verse 25).

- The Spirit helps us in our weakness (verse 26).

- And we know that in all things God works for the good of those who love him, who have been called according to his purpose (verse 28).

- If God is for us, who can be against us? (verse 31).

- Who shall separate us from the love of Christ? Shall trouble or hardship or persecution or famine or nakedness or peril or sword? (verse 35).

CHAPTER EIGHT

Loss

We had been married for years. So I was stunned when my wife, Jan, told me she wanted to go to counseling. Tearfully, she began to explain the sense of loss she felt from the sexual abuse she had experienced as a child. She had come to realize that she needed to deal with that loss.

Like a typical male, I had no idea what she was talking about. "Hey, if you've lost something, let's go find it." But I eventually realized she could no longer live with the unresolved issues surrounding her abuse. She was fighting depression, had relational issues in her family that no one had dealt with (and everyone quietly avoided), and she was unsettled in her head and heart.

So we started to go to counseling. We made the decision for her sake, but it soon became an opportunity for both of us. As I watched the counselor gently peel back the layers of emotion in Jan's life, I began to see how her loss had played such an integral role in her existence.

The counseling process lasted a year and a half. We drove two hours each way to spend two hours with a counselor. I loved that time…and hated it.

I loved learning how we both were wired and how various things in our lives had molded our thinking, behaviors, and interactions with others. But I hated the pain that came out of it, for her and for me, individually and as a couple. I learned so many things, including the way we handle loss by filling the emptiness with things that don't last. Jan's recognition of the futility of her efforts to fill those voids herself had finally moved her to a desperate point of pain, causing her to question her current state and to long for something different.

In my years of work with struggling teens and their families, I have seen this same thing over and over in young ladies who have been sexually abused. Let me give you an example of what I'm talking about.

Anna

Anna had been sexually abused by her grandfather for years. It started at age two and lasted until a seventh-grade slumber party, where one of Anna's friends heard her innocently share what her grandfather was doing to her. This sweet little friend told Anna that she should tell her mother. She did, and that was it. At least for a while.

As Anna matured, she began to realize what had really happened to her during those earlier years. And the older she got, the more furious she became. Not wanting to allow her grandfather to control her life, she exerted more and more effort to counteract the damage he had done to her. She wore herself out trying to prove she was something more than what her grandfather's abuse told her she was.

Every time he had committed an act of abuse, he had sent a message to Anna—a message that became clearer as the years passed. It was a message of disregard and disrespect, of deceit and brainwashing: "You're trash, and I can use you the way I want." This horrific luring of an innocent girl into a perverse world set into motion a way of thinking that almost destroyed this young sweetheart.

The response to this kind of abuse isn't what most would think. I learned years ago at a Hope for the Wounded Heart seminar by Dan Allender that girls can respond to sexual abuse by becoming party girls, bad girls, or good girls. Anna chose the good-girl route. She was compelled to prove that the message her grandfather had communicated countless times through the years was wrong. She was going to make herself perfect. She set out to be valued, adored, and honored.

But Anna didn't understand she couldn't do this by herself. All her efforts couldn't quite fill the emptiness that had been created by a selfish, uncontrolled man. As a result, she lived in a world of frustration and quiet rage, trying to erase the message she had received for years. She just couldn't quite do it.

I have come to believe that loss of any kind is one of the greatest motivators for behavior. It is why many teens do what they do. But this cause-and-effect style of living is a response to damage that's been done to us rather than a fulfillment of God's purpose in us.

God can use loss to our benefit. He takes what was meant for evil and uses it for good. But loss impacts how we live, and teens are no exception.

What Is Loss?

When I talk about loss, I am talking about those voids in life that come from not getting what you want, need, or hope for. Loss is the chasm in the heart caused by deprivation, by a failure to achieve something, or possibly by a defeat you experienced. It is the hollowness you are unable to overcome. It is a pit of loneliness that's left when something is taken away.

In times of loss, the gospel message is desperately needed. One of the greatest acts God can do for the person who has experienced loss is to fill the voids and chasms created by that loss and give the true freedom that comes only in a relationship with Christ.

The hole in Anna's life because of sexual abuse cannot be filled by anything she does or doesn't do. It can only be filled by God. How does He do it? I have no idea, but I know that He does. And when He does, Anna will no longer have to waste her time trying to fill it, time that she could have been spent fulfilling her purpose in life, acknowledging His thumbprint on her life, accepting the role He has called her to fill.

After one of our seminars, a 40-year-old fellow told me, "All my life I have lived to change one comment that was made to me when I was in sixth grade." A teacher had barked out a harsh remark that belittled and humiliated him in front of the class: "If you had as much brains as you do fat, you might make something of yourself!" Little did this teacher know that what she said would change the direction of a little boy's life in such a negative way.

He experienced a loss. Loss of value, respect, dignity, and honor. His thinking and behavior changed. He was committed to prove that teacher wrong, to show everyone else that he wasn't fat and that he was smart. He now lived with an "I'll show you" mentality. And he was controlled by an unknowing teacher and her rude comments rather than the One who created him.

As you read these words, did something said to you in your early years pop into your head? Perhaps your dad told you that you were stupid, or your mom said you were an embarrassment to the family. Maybe something was said that has been buried deep in your soul, but the sound of its message still rings in your head when you are still.

I don't really think that many people get through life without some type of loss…especially today's young people.

A father of one of the young men living with us at Heartlight shared how he spent most of his life responding to a comment his dad had made to him during his teen years. His dad never told him he was proud of him, and he stated many times that he didn't think his son would ever amount to much. He went on to share that he was now 50 years old, had done everything for his dad, but had accomplished nothing for God. He spent so much time trying to please his dad that he forgot he had been called to please his Father.

When Scripture tells us about the fruit of the Spirit in Galatians, the last on the list is self-control. I would submit to you that this last fruit may not be about just anger management or the squelching of lust. God does not want us to be controlled by things that could derail us from His intent and purpose for us. Self-control means not reacting to everything everyone has ever done to you, but responding to what He has done for you.

This is an important concept to grasp as you attempt to understand your teen's behavior. We've seen that behavior is driven by needs. So the question you need to ask is this: Has a loss in my child's life caused a need that his or her behavior is now trying to fill?

Scripture tells us that God is the spring of living water. You can drink all the water you want, but until you drink from Him, you will always thirst. My efforts to satisfy my needs will only temporarily satisfy my thirst. But His provision fully meets my need, ending my thirst and eliminating the need for me to find my own refreshment.

Jeremiah 2:13 (NIV) states it beautifully: "My people have committed two sins: They have forsaken me, the spring of living water, and have dug their own cisterns, broken cisterns that cannot hold water."

Moods of a Lifetime

Jan and I had the honor of living at a Christian sports camp in Branson named Kanakuk Kamp. We lived there for seven years back in the '80s. We had an incredibly wonderful time of learning as we rubbed shoulders with people from around the country and from all walks of life.

One of the joys of our time there was getting to know Spike and Darnell White. Spike was an 80-plus-year-old man who made everyone around him feel valuable. I had numerous opportunities to dive into deep discussions with Spike about why kids do what they do, what gets them off track, and how to work with kids who were struggling. I'll never forget a statement he made that appeared on much of the camp literature: "The moods of a lifetime are often set in the all-but-forgotten events of childhood."

Spike wanted people to provide great opportunities for kids that would help mold their character, their destiny, and their longings for life. His statement is undoubtedly true. But it has another side to it as well. Even forgotten events can cast a dark shadow over a person's life.

Jamie

Jamie was a young lady from Virginia who was shy, distrustful of people, self-centered, and protective in her conversations. She wanted to engage in deep, personal discussions, but she just couldn't because she couldn't trust anyone.

One day I asked her parents about her past. I asked a barrage of questions about her family, her social interactions, and her medical history. They shared that she had been adopted from Social Services in Richmond when she was one and a half years old. They knew that the time she spent with her birth parents was rough, but they assured me they didn't think that was the cause of her behavior because she didn't remember that time.

But then they described how traumatic her first one and a half years with them were. By the time she was three, she had to undergo surgery to repair rips and tears in her vagina because of sexual abuse from her birth father. When she was 18 months old, her birth father had intentionally broken her arm because she made a mess at dinner. They talked of her neglect and abuse, her medical conditions, and her suffering before Social Services intervened in the situation. Again, they assured me that she had no memory of any of the incidents.

While they were telling me this, my granddaughter, Maile, who was a year and a half at the time, was running around our conference center. I looked at her, imagining what damage would be done if I would do the same to her. I looked at the parents and asked, "Do you really think that all that has happened to Jamie has never affected her because she can't remember anything?" I then asked them, "What if I asked Maile to come over to me, and I grabbed her arm and broke it? Do you think she wouldn't remember it five years from now? And that it wouldn't affect her?" They were silent, and I thought, *Good night, you've got to be kidding me!*

Jamie had experienced great losses in her life. The loss of trust, innocence, safety, and protection, to name just a few, caused a mind-set that led to her current behaviors. The fact that she couldn't remember any of it doesn't mean that it didn't affect her.

The moods of a lifetime can also be set by the forgotten events in one's life.

Understanding Your Child's Loss

Every time I mention losses in any presentation I do, some parents ask, "What if we can't pinpoint any losses?" Good question.

I usually ask if they had losses during their early years. Most say yes. Then I ask, "Did your parents know about them?" Most say no. I then ask, "Could you perhaps not know everything that has happened to your child?"

The losses may not appear to be significant or remarkable. Remember when your child used to come to you and tell you, "Sally said I was stupid," and you countered it to reassure your child? "You're not stupid." "Don't listen to Sally; she doesn't know you." "Sweetheart, that's not true. You're one of the smartest people I know." Now jump ahead a few years to junior high. Does (or did) your child still tell you about those comments? Probably not.

Why? Because kids begin to believe some of those comments. And they won't come to us, so we must go to them. We must enter their world, asking what's going on in their lives, uncovering the hurts and pain they are experiencing.

Many stepparents don't understand why they sometimes aren't accepted by the new stepchildren. I often find that they remind the stepchildren of a loss. Something that once was is now gone. Something that should have been now can't be. The new stepmother is frustrated as she tries as hard as she can to connect with the new kids. She can't bridge the chasm between her and her new family because she reminds her stepkids of a loss—the loss of a mother, the loss of a stable home, the loss of a normal life.

So what is a parent or stepparent to do? Deal with the loss. In fact, dealing with the loss is more important than trying to change the behavior. Focus on the cause rather than the symptoms. David Damico, in his book *The Faces of Rage,* states, "Often repressed or forgotten, such childhood losses tend to re-emerge at significant transition points of change in the adult's life. This shows that unresolved loss is never resolved merely through the passage of time."[1] So, focus on dealing with the loss.

This is much easier when losses are pretty visible, such as the death of a parent, the loss of a loved one, a breakup, or the death of a friend. It's a little harder when the loss isn't visible and evident. But whether apparent or not, if your child is acting out, look hard for a loss he or she is trying to deal with.

What Does Loss Look Like?

For many young people, loss is often an *unmet expectation.* They believe things should be different than they are. They think people don't understand them, listen to them, or pay attention to them.

When children feel this way, they try to eliminate the loss or cover it up. But they don't know how to connect with peers, so the development of relationships is going to be the key to helping them through these tough times. More often than not, the relationship will be with a parent or other adult, not a peer.

Loss in kids' lives may also come as a result of the *actions of others.* When children experience this kind of loss, they are really paying for the foolish choices and behavior of other people. These losses include car accidents, others' mistakes, or situations where kids are the victims of others' bad judgments.

This loss can also come from abuse or neglect by parents or caregivers. When parents don't provide what a child needs, or when parents break the law and are caught, kids pay a price for the parents' willful selfish behavior. This type of loss may also come from societal prejudice, which has nothing to do with the children but has more to do with those who display their shortcomings with actions that damage.

Why is it important to know the various types of loss that a child would experience? Each type of loss creates a set of questions and issues that are far different from those generated by other losses. When kids are victims of others' bad choices, kids ask questions—not about other people or about themselves, but about life and about God:

- Why do bad things happen to good people?
- If God is such a loving God, why did He allow this to happen?

- If life is good, why do I always feel so bad?
- Why do I feel as if God doesn't like me?
- Is this part of God's will for my life?
- Why has God ignored me?
- Is life just a crapshoot?

Throughout my life I have heard the verse, "If God is for us, who can be against us?" But what if you're a young person who says, "No one is for me, and God is against me"? Kids need special help working through this kind of loss. They need spiritual discussions that will eventually bring hope to a dark time.

Another type of loss comes from *unfulfilled dreams* or postponed pursuits of something kids hope for. This kind of loss includes not reaching a goal or not taking advantage of an opportunity. It's not making the team, not getting the cheerleading spot, not being good enough to qualify for something that was so desperately desired.

This type of loss is focused inward and usually includes shame, guilt, and emptiness. When a young person has always believed in and hoped for something, but then realizes that it just isn't going to happen, reality is hard to swallow.

When a child realizes how things really are, parents might see a shutdown or a sudden shift in their child's interests. If this happens with your child, it's not the time to approach him or her with a discouraging comment like "I told you so," or "Well, you should've listened." Come alongside your child: "I know this is hard." Don't make it any less than what it is, and help your child not to make it any more than it is.

Finally, some losses are results of *uncontrolled outcomes* that affect children's lives. These tend to be situations kids must learn to accept as the way things are. It's a tough road. Avoid saying, "Well, that's just the way it is." Rather, be sensitive to your child and work hard at listening and hearing your child's heart. In these situations, your child will often feel like life just isn't fair, and no one can do anything about it.

Children may be forced to move to new city, leaving their friends behind. The losses may have been caused by natural disasters. And this is the category of loss an adopted child may experience—he or she has had no control over the placement.

By the way, a young person told me once that "adoption is the only trauma where we're expected to be thankful." Debate it all you want, but this young person is expressing a loss, and not judging a gain. All of us would do well to know the difference between the two.

Medical conditions, changes in personal appearance, and inherited afflictions can also create this kind of loss.

Response to Loss

A child's loss-free life is not an indicator of good parenting, nor is a loss-riddled life a sign of terrible parenting. The bumper sticker that says STUFF HAPPENS could just as easily say LOSS HAPPENS. It is inevitable. And wise parents understand their own loss and how that loss has affected them. And when they do, they are able to see the loss in their children's lives and move toward them to help them in difficult times.

Most kids will usually tell you that losses are really not that big of a deal. They minimize them, hoping to minimize the pain in their lives. I've had to break the news of a death to kids, and they'll respond by saying, "Well, I really didn't know her that well anyway," or "It's no big deal," or "I'm okay. I'm fine." Don't believe it.

I encourage you to give your children the freedom to respond to the hurt of any loss. They need to let off some emotional steam. That doesn't mean you allow a cavalcade of emotion to control your children and destroy your home. Just give your children permission to become undone once in a while, and as they express their pain, move toward them relationally.

When will children see their losses? Who knows! Maybe not for years. A young girl may realize her loss when she sees all the other girls with their dads and realizes she doesn't have one to hang out with her. Or a boy who tried out for the basketball team may feel the loss of being cut as he sits in the stands and watches others who made the team.

You may begin to feel a sense of loss when you begin to have a great relationship with your son or daughter, which reminds you that you never had that kind of relationship with your parents. I feel the loss of four kids who were dear to me whenever I hear the names Caroline, Todd, Cindy, or Darren. My wife remembers her loss whenever she smells Old Spice After Shave. Memories of losses can pop up anytime, anyplace, and be triggered by anything. And some of the behavior we see from young people can be their way to avoid or fill the void created by their loss.

Impact of Loss

Understanding loss doesn't give you all the answers to inappropriate and potentially dangerous behavior. But it does provide a different approach toward your children, even if *they* don't understand their loss. As we have seen, your child's behavior is not really the issue. It is just an indicator of the struggle that lies beneath the surface. Of course, you do need to deal with the behavior, or your child will continue on a path of destruction, spinning out of control.

As you gently probe your child's losses, you may stir the pain of your own losses. You might see that your response to loss has created some behavior patterns in you that are causing some pretty negative reactions from your spouse or kids. It's never too late to look at the log in your own eye. Introspection and reflection are acts of wisdom.

In fact, I believe that to deal with a child's loss, the parents need to understand the impact of loss in their own lives. I suggest you find someone to talk with about your life. Consider a counselor or a concerned pastor. Look for a women's or men's group where people can talk about their experiences and feelings. Keep looking until you find someone you can talk to about the things in your past that need some attention.

Loss is big in all our lives. And if you spend some time searching and understanding the damage that has occurred in your life, you might discover why certain people respond negatively to you in certain situations. And you may begin to understand what your child is going through.

Perhaps the damage in your life is getting in the way of your relationship with your child. Or perhaps you are transferring the damage in your life to your child. If either of those is true, you can begin a new process of healing.

I had never understood how my past losses impacted my thinking, behavior, and expectations until someone showed me the truth. I had avoided facing the damage done to me through life, and without other people's help I would never have seen it or known it existed.

People respond to losses in various ways, but the place to start when connecting with these people is always the same. You start where they hurt.

For instance, the teens that live with us at Heartlight probably can't tell you about their losses, but they can tell you where they hurt. We start by helping these kids through their pain in a setting where we can control their behavior. That environment gives them a chance to reflect on the damage that has been done to them, and as a result, they realize that loss plays a big part in their lives.

Most kids who have experienced loss feel like damaged goods. They will often spend the rest of their lives trying to feel whole again. Their self-value is diminished. Their selfishness compensates for their loss. They are confused about what life is supposed to be like (this is why most young people are so angry). And they begin to develop a style of relating to others that brings false and temporary value.

These kids begin the process of a slow death because they are driven by a selfish motivation to preserve what they have and to regain what they've lost. Avoidance becomes a priority of life, and their facade of value and confidence cloaks their pain and hurt.

These are tough days for teens. But they are also the best days to offer a message, a relationship, some wisdom, and perhaps a taste of something beyond themselves. Something that might touch their heart so that they catch a glimpse of a greater One who loves them more than they could ever imagine.

Losses can keep us from what God intends for us, prevent us from fulfilling our real purpose, and hinder our movement to become the people God desires us to be. Dealing with loss can consume us and take so much of our time that we never have time to become what we were intended to be.

Ephesians 2:10 (NIV) states, "For we are God's workmanship, created in Christ Jesus to do good works, which God prepared in advance for us to do." God has a plan and direction for each of our lives, and losses can cause a detour. They can move us away from His intent, His preparation, and His purpose. No wonder people are so frustrated in life and teens are so mad.

My wife wasn't created for her grandfather's enjoyment. Jamie wasn't created to suffer her father's abuse. Young men aren't supposed to grow up wondering whether they have more fat than brains. Moods of a lifetime aren't to be set by the damage done in our childhood by others. We weren't made for any of this.

That's why it is so important to understand the loss your child might be experiencing and to use that understanding to change your child's mind-set and behavior. To do otherwise only sets your child up for future pain and hardship.

> I will give thanks to You, for I am fearfully and wonderfully made; Wonderful are Your works, and my soul knows it very well (Psalm 139:14).

CHAPTER NINE

PUTTING YOUR KNOWLEDGE TO WORK

Wouldn't you love a quick fix for all the problems you have with your kids and in your home? Wouldn't you like to wake up one morning and find everything is different? Do you wish all the changes you'd like to see in your family could happen at the snap of a finger?

Sure you would. Wouldn't we all? But unfortunately, quick fixes never work.

Getting Your House in Order

As I mentioned very early in this book, chances are you're reading this book because something is not right. Or perhaps you think something might go wrong in your teen's life, and you're preparing yourself.

The first step is to get your house in order. It can still be relaxed, operating as planned chaos, but it must be in order.

Make no mistake. The plan of getting your house in order has to be strategic, deliberate, and calculated because the process of change takes time. But I have seen over and over that if parents will develop a plan, most homes will quickly begin moving toward health. Let me offer an effective approach to making changes in your home:

Identify the Things That Must Change

Let me ask you a question: If your children continue to do the same things they're doing now, where will your family be in five years? If you don't like the answer, then something must change between now and then. So wouldn't today be a good day to get started? What would you like to see changed? What would you like to be different?

Sit down with a pad of paper and write down what you like in your home and what you don't like. And while writing, don't let the problems you have caused get in the way of the changes you want to see. Just because you haven't been a perfect parent doesn't mean you can't require some changes. Everything is constantly changing; your child is getting older, new opportunities arise, your family is exposed to new things, and you're becoming wiser.

You need to understand you are not bound by what you did or didn't do years earlier—or by mistakes you made in your early years that you can no longer reverse. You should no longer have to "do time." Forgiveness includes giving up hope that you'll ever have a better past. It's time to move on. Don't be afraid to list those things that are wrong. You may be numb to some of them, but that doesn't mean they are okay. Change cannot begin until we accept that a problem exists.

Set the Stage for Change

Nothing is wrong with sitting down with your children and sharing with them that your family needs to make some changes. And even if you know what those changes should be, just say "I'm not sure what needs to change, but something needs to change."

I would also ask them what they would like to see changed in your family or your home. Whatever they say, try not to respond unless asked. Wait until they say, "Well, Mom (or Dad), what would you like to see changed in our home, in our family?" Don't answer. Tell them, "Good question…let me think about it." If you answer, you'll take away their chance to think for themselves about what might need to change.

Implementing your kids' suggestions is usually far better than implementing your own. You might say, "You know, guys, you're no longer kids, and I think we treat you like kids too much," and leave it at that.

"Come on, Dad. What do you mean?"

"I don't know....I just think we shouldn't treat you like little kids anymore." See what's happening? You're setting the stage for change.

You can tell them that "Mom can't continue to do this anymore," or "I know things have been kind of strained, and I want things to be different," or "Guys, we have a problem, and something's gotta give," or just a statement that says, "I think I'm losing you, and I can't stand back and do nothing." This one is tough because, of course, a child will ask "What do you mean?" Don't answer, but say, "I don't know, I just feel like I'm losing you." You are helping them get ready for change before you share what the problem is.

Prepare Your Family for Change

After you have spent some time setting the stage (perhaps a week later), begin to communicate the problems you see in your home and family. Don't dump everything at once! Start with just a couple things.

Perhaps the main issue in your home is disrespect. You could say, "Son, let's get together and discuss what I mentioned last week." If he doesn't want to get together, take something away that is important to him, like the car, cell phone, computer, PlayStation, Xbox, or whatever it takes to get his attention. He may yell, "That's manipulation!" And you can say, "That's right, but that's how important it is for us to talk. So when do you want to get together?" And then suggest a time.

If he's still not ready, don't push it yet. But if he continues to balk, take more away. Let him see that more pain will come until you and he sit down and talk. You're forcing his hand.

This may be a new stance for you, particularly if you're a single parent. Single parenting is tough. It is usually born of loss. And that shared loss moves parent and child together. An easy way to survive is for the parent and the kids to become peers. But the single parent will have a hard time moving back into the parent role—the role of the authority—especially if that parent has just gotten remarried. But it's a necessary and important move when you have to confront issues in your home.

Communicate the Change

Now you can begin to implement the changes. Begin by communicating what you want to see changed. You can say, "Here are the changes, and this is what we'd like to see different." You may have allowed some attitudes or actions in your family that are now no longer acceptable, and now is your opportunity to say, "We were wrong."

Implement the Plan

This is your chance to use what you learned from the first chapters of this book. You learn when to be strong and when to be sensitive. You learn to allow your kids to go through some temporary pain in order to learn the consequences of inappropriate behavior. This is when parents—whether together, separated, or divorced—should implement the plan in one accord.

This is also the *crucial* time when your children will determine just how serious you are about change. They will assess your genuineness and dedication to the process of getting your house in order. And they will learn whether you are capable of following through on what you have said and whether you truly believe in what you are doing.

Establishing a belief system is one of the best ways to communicate what you would like your home to look like. I will discuss this in a later chapter.

Do these five steps sound easy? In some situations, yes. In others, no.

Breaking a horse sounds easy. The actual process is grueling, as anyone who has worked with horses would testify. Rarely do family members all agree in the initial stages of implementing new ideas that will cause pain, discomfort, or uneasiness. But on the other side of all these temporary symptoms you will find deeper relationships and healthier people.

The Foolish, the Wise, and the Repentant

We would be foolish to believe we must achieve happiness on our own terms without consideration of or dependence on God, our families, or anyone else. We are foolish when we are so convinced we are right, we won't listen when others try to help. Foolish people believe they can handle everything if everyone will just leave them alone.

Foolishness is self-centeredness at its apex and selfishness in all its glory.

Foolishness leads to more and more pain. And unless someone else gets involved, a foolish person usually won't turn around and come to his senses until he is eating out of a garbage can on some back alley.

Scripture tells us that "foolishness is bound up in the heart of a child; the rod of discipline will remove it far from him" (Proverbs 22:15). Of course, this doesn't mean that you should beat a child into changing. Your "rod of discipline" might be the car keys. It might be a grounding. It might be other consequences or privileges taken away. It's not necessarily just physical punishment.

People tell me all the time that these young people "just need their clock cleaned a couple times" and they'd straighten up. They do need to feel pain and discomfort, but pain doesn't come only in the form of corporal or physical punishment.

Then they say, "Well, it worked for me, it should work for them. I mean, you train horses the same way you did a hundred years ago, don't ya?"

My answer? No. And my child isn't a horse. The world is completely different than it was 20 years ago. The culture has changed. Kids' opportunities have changed. Their possessions have changed. Their amount of exposure to stuff has changed. Their style, their likes and dislikes, and their interactions have changed. Getting whacked with a leather belt just doesn't work anymore.

The issue at hand, and the encouragement of Scripture, is not that you need to take a rod to your children. Rather, you need to use some form of discipline with your children to get them to stop what they're doing because they will damage their lives if they continue.

So use any type of rod of discipline you want, but have the courage to use something. Any rod of discipline will create pain and discomfort in the lives of your children and move them in a new direction. And when they move on to something else, you hope and pray they will make a wiser choice than the choice they have been making.

And how are they going to get input for that next choice? From you, Mom. From you, Dad.

In contrast to foolishness, wisdom is the application of principles of right living gained through observation, reflection, and experience. What my children watch, what they think about, and what they do will give them opportunities to gain wisdom to make better choices and healthier decisions.

Here comes a set of questions that might bite a little. What do your children observe? What do they think about? What has been their experience? And how do you help them gain wisdom?

Kids probably won't like you when you begin to get your house in order, but they will love you for your stand and for your willingness to stand up to them for something better. And the momentary pain that change creates is a small price to pay for the greater reward of helping a child mature and gain wisdom by not allowing childish behavior to continue.

Use temporary discomfort to move your child to repentance and change. By the way, I define *repentance* as the recognition of false images and beliefs related to meeting personal needs and the forsaking of those images and beliefs for a commitment to and dependence on God, your family, and others.

Most parents want change within their family but don't know what to do. Or they want change but do nothing because they are afraid of their children's responses. As a result, the children control their home, determine the atmosphere in which everyone lives, and thwart any attempt to have some type of order. And parents usually get numb to their children's behavior and retreat from the relationship, which only allows their children to continue on their path of destruction. The parents don't even realize the level of depravity their children have moved to and silently watch their children deteriorate, beginning other behaviors of coping that have even worse consequences.

Here are three stories of parents who decided to get their houses in order and exercise some discipline. These parents were determined to stop their children's destructive behavior and help them learn that what they were doing was unacceptable.

Angel

Angel was a 16-year-old girl who chose to simply ignore her mom and dad. Even when they tried to create an opportunity for discussion or when they would confront her, Angel would belittle and demean. She verbally attacked her parents...and then silence. She used a litany of abuses to shut down everything Mom or Dad would say.

"Deal with it, Dad."

"Shut up, Mom. You can't tell me what to do."

"You guys are so wrong. Who do you think you are?"

"Screw you, Dad! I'm leaving."

"Why do you always point the finger at me when you're just as screwed up?"

"Why don't you look in the mirror?"

"Get over it, nobody's perfect."

"I can't wait until I can leave this house!"

Whenever Mom or Dad tried to talk to Angel and tell her that some things were wrong, she glared at one of them, rolled her eyes, and then walked away in disgust, acting as if Mom and Dad weren't even in the room. Her most famous act was to put in her ear buds from her iPod and turn up the music when Mom started talking to her, thus drowning Mom out. Not exactly behavior that would get her the Miss Congeniality award from *Today's Family!*

When I first met Angel and watched her unleash one of her volleys of verbal trash toward her parents, I wondered, *How did this young lady ever get named Angel?* (I think I could have come up with a more appropriate name.) I chuckled inside while watching this 16-year-old girl try to appear to be above us all. She was in fact reducing herself to something quite lower than most kids I've seen.

For some reason, Angel's style of relating to her parents was working for her. Her foolishness was extreme and her demeanor was loud. And if someone didn't stop it, she was headed to a place in her relationships she didn't want to go. No wonder this young lady had no friends and couldn't hold a job. She was so offensive she pushed people away.

After meeting with Angel's parents, I asked if they were ready for things to get worse. Placing some requirements around Angel would probably result in more intense attacks. They were scared to death. They knew they had to do something, but they were so fearful of her response that they froze up and just walked away.

I met with them just a few times to help them put together a mini belief system for their house, only focusing on a few things that needed to change. Our goal was to keep Angel from having to move out. I prefaced the belief system with these instructions:

1. Write down three things you would like to see changed in Angel's behavior.
2. Put those things into a letter and give it to her. (Discussion wasn't getting anywhere.)
3. In the letter, set a time to spend 30 minutes to talk about it. Mom or Dad will do all the talking.
4. Whatever the response, drop it. This isn't the time to prove you are serious. That comes later. Now is the time to say, "No more," and "This is where we stand."

Here is our mini belief system:

1. Angel must immediately stop disrespectfully ignoring Mom and Dad.
2. Angel must immediately stop her cutting comments and accusations.
3. Even if Angel rejects Mom and Dad, they will never reject her. Dad (or Mom) will eat breakfast with Angel once a week at a restaurant of her choice.
4. Any violation or disregard for the above will result in consequences including Mom and Dad taking away the car, not paying insurance, and taking away the cell phone.

Angel may have to ride the bus to school (or walk), she might not receive money for clothes, and she could lose the computer and the iPod.

5. Angel will not belittle or display arrogance or meanness toward anyone in the family. (The school would need to deal with issues at school, and her friends would have to deal with her on that level.)

Angel's parents handed her the letter, and her first comment was, "What's this?" They told her it was just a letter outlining some things they'd like to see different in the home. She tore it in half, threw it down, and stormed out of the house. Mom and Dad called me, and I told them to just put the torn letter on her pillow for her to read later that night. They did.

She came home, read the letter, and stormed into their room. She couldn't ignore this. Her volley began, and they just listened. When she was finished, Dad, who must have been given a divine inspiration, just said, "It starts tomorrow."

Angel was pretty calm the next few days. When I had my conversation with her parents, I told them, "That's what they said about Mount St. Helens a few days before the explosion. Just wait." After three days, her old style returned, and Mom and Dad now had to decide whether to follow through. They did, and Angel's response was the same as before. But this time, it was in disbelief that Mom and Dad were actually going to do something.

Like training horses, once you start disciplining your child, you can't stop, or the behavior will only get worse. Angel's comments and ignoring behavior continued, as did the subsequent loss of privileges, for three months. And then she finally got the picture. The breakfasts were pretty quiet for the next couple of months. But as it would any teen, uncomfortableness moved Angel to want to talk rather than be silent. And because her parents had been consistent with the consequences in the previous months, she began to engage rather than belittle.

The three months of pain—for everyone—were beginning to pay off. A new day was dawning with the beginnings of a real relationship between Angel and her parents. Angel and I even laughed together at the way she acted during all the conflict. I called her DD for "Devil in Disguise," and it's still a comment I jokingly remind her of whenever we talk.

Charlie

Charlie was 17 and a hermit. He buried his head in the sand of his room. He was disconnected, disengaged, and disassociated from everyone and everything. Something was overwhelming him, and his mom couldn't figure out what it was. She and I talked about him not doing well in school, missing classes, and somehow getting into college someday.

When I finally met with Charlie (which he agreed to only because his mother threatened to take away his DVD player in his room), he seemed like a pretty neat young man. But something was stirring below the surface that he wouldn't talk about and I couldn't get to.

He wasn't aggressive—actively or passively. Nor was he verbally abusive. This sounded more alarms for me than more intense behavior would have. He was just despondent and in despair. I wasn't concerned about what Charlie might be doing; I was concerned that he was doing nothing. Usually kids want something, but he didn't. Most are motivated toward something, but he wasn't.

The only things that Charlie cared about were his guitar, his DVD player, his computer games, and his cat, Dork. At this point, school, friends, activities, privileges, and possessions meant nothing. Oddly, he wasn't depressed. He was completely happy to just live in his room and exist.

He wouldn't eat meals with his sister and mother. And he wouldn't get out of bed until noon. He just didn't care. And if anyone tried to talk to him about where he was headed, he just started crying and quit talking.

Oddly, Charlie and his mom had a great relationship. But she protected him, enabling him to live in his own world, which wasn't going to change unless someone forced that change.

My counsel to Charlie's mom was pretty simple:

1. Take the blinds off the bedroom windows.
2. Tell Charlie that he's going to have to go to a counselor if he wants to keep his DVD player and computer.
3. Explain to Charlie that if he wants to flunk out of school he can, but he can't be at home during the day when she is not there. (This meant she would probably have to change the locks.)
4. If he doesn't go to school but wants to live at home, he has to get a job.
5. All meals are to be eaten in the kitchen with everyone else.

Pretty simple counsel, huh? But these five steps are not the end of the process. Taking the blinds off the bedroom windows was a tactic to show that change was coming, and it allowed the sun to start the waking process. The counselor suggested medication, but the responsibility to take it was Charlie's if he was to continue to live at home.

Getting him out of the house rocked his world and changed his environment. Even hanging out at Starbucks forced interaction with other people and gave the counselor some pretty easy topics to discuss. His new job showed him the value of people more than it did the value of money. And making him eat meals at the table with everyone else forced interaction and eliminated his reclusive existence.

We chose each of the requirements to produce actions that we hoped would take Charlie to a different place. The difficulty was getting Mom to quit enabling this young man. Changing her ways was painful for her. It forced her to try something new and to get her house in order. But the pain she endured probably saved her son's life. All it took was a little encouragement and a clear understanding of what she wanted for her son.

Tracy

Tracy was a 15-year-old who yelled, screamed, and cussed like a sailor when her parents tried to correct or discipline her. Her style wasn't to ignore or shut down. She attacked with a vengeance.

She developed this response mechanism to avoid receiving input. And her tantrums reminded her of her behavior when she was a six-year-old. If Mom or Dad tried to correct her while they were on vacation, out to dinner, or at church, life got ugly real fast. Needless to say, anyone would want to avoid a situation like that.

Which is exactly what people did. They avoided her—in every way. They feared being put in an embarrassing situation.

Tracy's parents didn't have to ask what the problem was—it was always in their face. Both parents started working more, spending more time together, working out more, and keeping busier at church, probably to avoid their daughter, which only fueled Tracy's anger and verbal abuse.

This young lady was a poison and one of the most demanding, self-centered, self-absorbed, arrogant, pathetic young ladies I've ever met. But something was also pretty special about her. She was kind to animals and loved little children, and when she wasn't yelling and screaming, she was very thoughtful. I knew something was triggering her behavior. To stand up to this young lady would be too much of a challenge for many people. I applauded her parents for their patience and willingness to do battle.

My counsel to them was to find out what her favorite activities and possessions were. This would help determine the rewards and consequences for her behavior. Tracy's parents needed to help her realize that she would suffer penalties for anything not age appropriate, but she would be rewarded for meeting their standards for 30 days. And that reward would be something she's always wanted.

Tracy's habit had become part of her character. It was a coping skill she had acquired, unchallenged by Mom and Dad, and it was working for her. Because her parents had allowed it for so long, it was fully engrained in her personality.

I encouraged the family to hold to what was right and get prepared for the long haul of battles, confrontations, consequences, and turmoil. These were difficult, but Tracy eventually learned that she needed to change. That process included stopping one behavior and learning a new behavior.

Tracy had lived with this behavior for so long that progress came very slowly. In fact, her parents didn't see any progress at all for more than a year. Tracy took a year and a half to win her first reward. Eventually, the "long obedience in the same direction" finally broke Tracy of the patterns that would have destroyed her relationships if her parents had allowed them to continue.

What's Normal Behavior Anymore?

Parents say to me all the time that they don't know what's normal anymore. Here are some behaviors I think are pretty normal. But remember, though they may be normal, some are unacceptable.

- Not wanting to do chores—and wanting everyone else to do things for them.
- Enjoying doing those same chores for other families.
- Putting off chores and then wanting to be paid for doing them.
- Showing anger when they don't get what they want.
- Forgetting to mow the yard and then writing their girlfriend's name in the yard with the lawnmower when they do decide to mow.
- Maintaining a ransacked room.
- Putting off homework until they want to do it.
- Not wanting to go to bed—and not wanting to get out of it in the morning.
- Talking on their cell phone forever and saying nothing.
- Not wanting to call anyone to find a job.
- Losing their retainer or contacts, breaking glasses, ripping shirts.
- Not caring about brushing their teeth but wanting them to be as white as everyone's in the commercials.
- Not liking who they are and who you are. Wanting everyone else to be like them while they try to be like everyone else.

- Telling you what you want to hear and swearing that nobody listens.
- Forgetting to thank people for gifts they've received.
- Not wanting to go to church.
- Demanding more free time and later curfews and swearing no one else has a curfew.
- Being unsatisfied with any parenting skills you might possess.
- Wanting to be different while trying to be like everyone else.
- Making an occasional bad grade and not caring about making good grades.
- Wanting to be faddish and stylish even when the look might counter what they really believe.
- Not thinking about college until right before the application deadline.
- Hating things today they loved yesterday and vice versa—including you.
- Wanting things but not wanting to work for them.
- Not wanting to appear in public with their parents, but wanting parents to finance their public appearances.
- Indulging in occasional outbursts of anger.
- Choosing actions that are more curious and experimental than adoptive and lifelong.
- Not knowing what they want to do as a career.
- Loving music as a means to identify with others rather than because of what it says.
- Saying stupid things that are best left alone and unnoticed.
- Wanting to just waste time with friends but really feeling like it's a waste of time hanging with Mom and Dad.
- Longing to be told they are loved by someone.
- Wanting some security and significance from parents.
- Anxious to get older but never wanting to grow up.

It's the nature of the beast. Don't try to change that nature. You can't. It's called adolescence, and it comes with its own set of behaviors. You don't have to accept and allow all of these tendencies, but you might enjoy knowing that almost all teens struggle with these things.

When to Take a Stand

Some situations are not normal and prompt you to get your house in order. Some parents slide into situations without realizing the mess they're in until it's so bad, they can't dig themselves out. That's when some quit.

This downward slide happens over a long period of time when inappropriate behaviors are gradually accepted. And it normally happens very slowly.

I often hear parents describe their situation at home, justifying and excusing potentially dangerous and deadly behaviors. I have to stop them in the conversation and say, "Let me repeat back to you what you're telling me, and you tell me if you think this is all right." They usually look somewhat aghast as I reflect back to them what I heard them say.

Sometimes parents see only the good in their children. They fail to see what's going wrong and are usually caught off guard when they realize what's happening.

Let me list some behaviors that demand immediate attention and that are clear indicators that you need to get your house in order. These behaviors are not normal for teens.

- A sudden change in personality and rejection of normal things.
- A change in friends, association with those you never wanted your child to hang around.
- Outbursts of anger that include profanity and show extreme disrespect.
- Extreme need for sleep.
- A depressed nature that expresses itself in dark thoughts,

inability to get out of bed, sporadic crying for no apparent reason, and ever-increasing risk taking.

- Sexual activity.
- Use of drugs, alcohol, or marijuana.
- Getting physical with anyone in the family, including punching, hurting, or beating the family pet.
- Avoidance of any interaction with family.
- Hurting oneself, including self-mutilation or cutting.
- Failing grades or unwillingness to go to school.
- Extreme rebellion, verbal abuse, aggressive behavior, or disrespect for family and friends.
- Dishonesty and disobedience as character traits.
- Defiance to the standards of the home and the values of the family.

This is not meant to be an exhaustive list, but these behaviors represent the major areas that may indicate the need for correction. In some cases, professional help might be of utmost importance and necessity.

Knowing what is normal and what is not can help you determine what you need to focus on for your home and family. Don't be afraid to do what is right.

CHAPTER TEN

The Importance of a Belief System

One of the great mistakes many parents make is not establishing a belief system when their kids are young. Such a system is crucial if your home is to operate effectively. Let me explain what I mean and demonstrate the impact such a system can have.

A belief system includes a list of what you believe, a set of rules for how your family will function based on your beliefs, and consequences for breaking the rules. This ensures that when inappropriate behavior occurs, the consequences have already been determined. Such a system should provide you with a relational policy and procedure manual for your home.

By putting a belief system into place, you are able to correct mistakes you've made, effectively address new issues when they surface, and get control of situations that can spin or are currently spinning out of control. And you can create an atmosphere where relationships can flourish.

Adolescence often catches a family a little unprepared, causing parents to feel inadequate in managing their home. And if organization is ever crucial, it's during the adolescent years. That's why establishing a belief system as early as possible is so important.

Having said that, I should add that it's never too late to put such a system into place.

Even if you have a belief system, adolescence often calls for updated and renewed rules. The beginning of difficulties with your teen demands a set of rules that clearly outlines the path you want to follow and the path you *don't* want to follow.

Most people don't plan on having problems, so they don't prepare for them. As a result, they haven't figured out how to respond until those problems are upon them. A belief system for your home allows you to prepare for the adolescent years and the challenges and problems they bring. It provides a road map with directions to follow and outlined consequences for getting off track.

Don't misunderstand. This isn't just a static list of rules that allows you to disconnect from your child by pointing to the refrigerator (where you have this posted) when your child steps out of line. It is a communication tool that gives defined goals, desires, and expectations to your child and then backs those up with rules and consequences. A belief system communicates to your child, "Let's go this way, and I'll go with you" instead of "That's the way you need to go, and I'll stand over here and watch."

My son gave me a Father's Day card last year that had an anonymous quote: "The successful man leads where others follow, persists where others give up, speaks softly while others may shout, listens when others may not, and lives from both his head and his heart." I believe by giving this process a little thought and time, developing such a path for your family will allow you to live from your head and your heart.

I tell my staff that when they have an idea about how we should operate Heartlight, they should write it down. Something about writing down thoughts and organizing them begins to line out a clear path to follow. Writing out your belief system lines out a clear path for your kids, but more importantly, it lines it out for you as a parent.

Why is it so important to have things lined out and not just shoot from the hip? Here's why: Everything you put into play with your teen will be questioned. These questions might require answers if your teens are to follow your lead.

"Why?"

"Come on, Dad, that's stupid."

"I'm not following those rules."

"Who do you think you are, telling me what to do?"

"Why do we have to do that?"

"You gotta be kidding me!"

"You're not going to tell me how to live."

"What do you mean, *rules?* I've been happy without them."

"Did Mom put you up to this?"

"Who died and made you God?"

"I'll go live with Dad. He doesn't have rules like this!"

"No one else's parent is doing this."

"Come on, Mom, what's the big deal?"

How to Develop a Belief System

If your child is spinning out of control and every morning you wake up asking, *Lord, prepare me for whatever is going to happen today,* you are ripe for establishing a belief system. Such a system is vital when you wonder what's next with your teens—whether you will discover they have been stealing, whether they are using drugs or alcohol again, whether your son had sex last night again with his girlfriend, or whether he'll be in school today. Many parents of out-of-control kids spend so much time trying to get a handle on all the problems that they don't have time to set up a system of rules and consequences, much less even think of what they believe. If you're caught in one of these situations, let me show you how to set up a belief system for your home. This is where the system is most useful. If your home is spinning out of control, it will help you regain control.

Begin by asking yourself, *What do I want, and what would I like to see changed in my home?* Call it a brainstorming session. Call it a dream. Call it whatever you want, but it's the first step in getting your house in order.

The best way to answer these questions is to state your beliefs. A teen will expose your beliefs. And if your beliefs can stand the scrutiny of adolescence, where things are challenged, violated, and complained about, then those truths and beliefs will probably hold true, and your kids will ultimately adopt them.

Beliefs About Your home

Beliefs are those convictions, opinions, ideals, morals, and values that you hold dearly because of your experience, biblical wisdom, tradition, culture, or marriage.

So if you had to put together a Top Ten list of what you believe about your home, what would you write down? Might I suggest some things to consider that I believe are important? As you go through these, don't think of rules to put with them yet. Just think about what you would like to see.

Academics. What kind of grades do your kids need to make? Are you going to pay for college? Do your children get to choose where they want to go? Do they have to carry a full load at school? What if they skip class? Or get in trouble at school? What course of action will you take if they begin to flunk a class?

Spiritual. Are you going to require your kids to go to church? Do they have to go to Sunday school? Young Life? Camp during the summer? Sunday night church? Wednesday night Bible study? Is there a time when they can miss? During their senior year, do you allow them to make the choice of what to do? Do they have to go on the summer mission tour with the church? What do you do if they hate church? Do they only get to hang out with church kids?

Social. What kind of curfew are you going to set? When will they be allowed to date? What is that process of dating? Can they stay over at others' homes? Do you have to meet the other parents? What if you disapprove of their friends? Do you have a say in who they can hang out with? Are you going to allow them to go hang out at the mall? Will you let them go on the senior trip? How many nights a week can they be out? Do they have to check in during the night? What if they don't come in one night? What if they're late? Do they only group date? Can they go on a trip with the opposite sex?

Behavioral. Are you going to allow disrespect? Do dishonesty and disobedience call for punishment? What is acceptable and unacceptable behavior? Will you allow your kids to drink, pierce something, or tattoo something on their bodies? How will you allow them to dress? What do you believe about smoking? Drinking? Drugs? Sex? Will you allow extreme sports like parachuting, bungee jumping, or motocross? What do you believe about teenage pregnancy? What if your child runs away? What if he or she wrecks the car or gets a ticket? What do you think about driving while on the cell phone?

Character. What character traits would you like to see your children develop? How will you help these grow? How do you want your daughter to present herself in a seductively dressed world, and what will you allow? Do you want your child to have a job? Will sports be required? What kind of work should kids do around the house? How serious is extreme disrespect? What happens when you catch your son in a lie? Who handles the discipline in the family?

Medical. If your child is on medication, are you responsible to make sure he or she takes it? If you have a special-needs child, how will that affect each family member's responsibilities? What if your children don't take care of their teeth? What if a retainer is lost? Who pays for broken glasses? Who pays for new contacts?

Possessions. How tidy must your kids' room be? Beds made? Where is the computer going to be placed in the home? Who buys the clothes? Who approves the clothes? What kind of games will you allow? Cell phone? Pager? Car?

Entertainment. What kind of music will you allow your child to listen to? What ratings of videos and movies are okay? What concerts will you allow them to go to? Which TV programs are okay, and which ones are not? Are cuss words in songs allowable? Rap?

Responsibilities. Who's going to do the laundry? Should kids help with meals and cleanup? Who's going to pick up the other younger siblings from school? How much time needs to be given to help out around the house? Are chores required? What are they? Are you going to give allowance? Who pays car insurance? Who holds the title to the car your kids drive? Will you require your kids to tithe? Do Mom and Dad have a say in where they can work and where they can't?

Privileges. Will you purchase your kids a car when they're 16? When do they get to start making choices? And about what?

Family. Do you have any requirements for family time? How often must the whole family have dinner together? How would you like to see your family members treat one another? Do you need to spell out any blended-family issues?

With so many things to get a handle on, you may be thankful for birth control. Whew! Did you ever think you would have to consider so much? And these are just the questions that you *know* you'll have to answer. Who knows what surprises and other challenges you'll face?

Perhaps you aren't clear about your beliefs...and perhaps this is the reason everything seems so chaotic and crazy in your home. So why not start now to put things in order? As you do, let me give you just a few other things to consider.

Do Beliefs Change?

Yes, I think beliefs do change. Over time, most people change what they believe. I'm not talking about shifting with the culture or justifying sinful behavior. Rather, I'm suggesting we check to make sure we're realistically applying the unchanging truth to our ever-changing lives.

I used to believe some pretty crazy things:

- Toilet seats transmit diseases.
- Vietnam was a good thing.
- Presidents of the United States could never do anything wrong.
- Guys with earrings were gay.
- Rock 'n' roll was evil.
- You had to have a few scars from gunshot wounds and stabbings to be a Harley rider.
- All Christians were Republicans.
- California was the land of fruits and nuts.

- If you did all the right things, your child would always do well.

- I could ride anything mechanical or alive.

- My children would always listen to me.

- I'd never be fired from a job.

- I could always trust people.

- A family that prayed together, stayed together.

- Bad things didn't happen to good people.

- If I slapped someone on the back while their eyes were crossed, they'd stay that way (my brother still has bruises, and his vision is fine).

Do beliefs change? You bet they do. So let me ask a tough question: Is what you believe rooted in something that isn't right? Because if it is, you're going to be confronted with it when you bring it up to your kids. And you're going to have some explaining to do. I'm not challenging your belief, but I want you to be prepared to defend what you truly believe.

What I thought I would have done, I didn't. And what I promised would happen, hasn't. And in many instances, I'm glad.

I've had numerous parents tell me they always told their daughter if she ever got pregnant she would have to leave the house. In more than 30 years of working with kids who've gotten pregnant, I've yet to meet a family that has followed through with that statement. Not one dad has kicked his daughter out of the house because she was pregnant. Rather, I've seen parents set aside this unhelpful position so they could help their daughter during her most difficult time.

Without a plan, good intentions fail. And using an outdated plan to tackle current issues is a disaster in the making. Your beliefs might be in order, but your plan may not. Take some time to clarify your primary beliefs and determine whether you have an effective plan for incorporating those beliefs into your family life.

Rick and Vicki

I've performed over 300 weddings of kids who've lived with us through the years, so I have the opportunity to see the long-term effects of what we do. One of the weddings I performed years ago was for a girl named Vicki.

Vicki recently called with some questions about their sons, who are 14, 17, and 18 years old. The 18-year-old lives at home and is attending a junior college. Vicki's husband, Rick, loves the boys dearly and feels the need to have family devotions. He has built this desire into the makeup of their home for years.

But as the boys moved into their teen years, their mind-set became quite different from what it was in their elementary school years. The boys began to question everything. They challenged the style of the devotions. They thought that watching children's videos and having a discussion time was no longer appropriate.

Their rebellion against Dad and his ways of doing family devotions caused so much friction in the home that the boys began to lose their relationship with their best friend. And Dad was getting angrier and angrier as the days passed. Rick began to lose the enjoyment of being with his three best buds and felt frustrated most of the time as a result of his kids' disrespect. Rick struggled to hear what his sons were telling him, and he hadn't learned to stop a good thing when it had run its course.

Family devotions can be wonderful. Rick's desire to build eternal perspectives into his kids pleases God. But Rick's approach was wrong. His sons weren't learning the way they used to. They longed for something different, and they felt as if they were being treated like little kids.

Great concept but poor delivery. Good belief but bad strategy. Perhaps the family needed a break from the devotions. Maybe the activity could be done a different way. Maybe what was a good idea at one time is no longer a good idea. If having devotions is destroying relationships, then it's time to evaluate whether it is indeed a good thing.

Things change. And so must you.

Pick Your Battles

You could probably come up with 100 different ways you'd like to see your home operate differently. But implementing all 100 of those new ideas would overwhelm everyone. You need to pick a few items that are the most important for you to tackle now and add more later.

I always believed a family should go to church together. When my children grew into their high school years, they didn't like the church we were going to, so we decided to go to the church they wanted to attend. It was where all their school friends went. Quite honestly, the church drove me nuts. It just wasn't the place that Jan and I felt we should be. We had to choose between going to church as a family and going to churches that were right for each of us.

I shifted. We decided to let them go to their church while we went to ours, and we met for lunch immediately following. Did I no longer believe that a family should go to church together? No, I still do. But I couldn't force our kids to be happy at our church, and I couldn't force myself to be happy at theirs, so we decided this wasn't a battle worth fighting.

As I get older, I let go of some of the things that I thought were important so I can focus on some wiser truths, some more intelligent understandings, and perhaps some more sensible beliefs. Sometimes I have been stuck in the past, enjoying the way things used to be. That rarely works as family members grow.

Setting the Rules

Once you have identified a few beliefs your family can build on, you can formulate rules that will help you live out those beliefs. Rules are boundaries that apply the beliefs and define what is acceptable and what is not.

Some teens will be relieved to have rules established, as most young people I meet like knowing the boundaries they can operate within. Others struggle as their parents suddenly erect fences where the kids have been allowed to roam free.

Many parents fail to set the rules of the house because they fear their children's responses. If you are one of those parents, you have a choice to make. You can continue to live in fear of your child, hoping the sense of intimidation you feel will go away, or you can take a stand and face your fear head-on.

Remember, behavior can be changed. Your kids may make an initial outburst, but their response will eventually change as you put your rules in place and begin to enforce them.

Setting rules will draw a line in the sand. If their response is as negative as you anticipate, it will only prove the need for the rules. Of course, this would be one of the first rules for a home like this: Everyone in the family must feel safe and be free from emotional outbursts that damage relationships and cause them to live in fear.

The establishment of rules ushers in a time of change and transition. The first response is usually negative, and that's usually the first change you have to work on. But given time, and by offering more to your family, the new rules will create a healthier atmosphere where most kids can flourish. Sure, some teens flounder a bit, but don't let that keep you from creating a healthy family environment.

Everyone can adjust. Everyone can adapt.

People often ask me what happens when children cannot adapt to the new system, and their negative and inappropriate behavior escalates. My answer is simple: The child cannot continue to live at home. Why? Because no one person is more important than the family. And to allow one person to remain in the home who is willfully and deliberately destroying the family or himself is a great disservice to others in the home.

When you let children know you will not allow them to continue such behavior, you make a critical statement: This family is worth fighting for, and nothing will stand between us to keep us from being where God desires us to be. I'll discuss this more in a later chapter.

Establishing Consequences

Now that you have established the rules, you need to set in place consequences. Consequences are actions brought about by breaking the rules you have established. Consequences are not just a way to punish for negative behavior. They are designed to direct your child toward a better life.

Consequences can be the loss of various things:

- participation in certain activities (nights out, prom, date night, movie night, youth group)
- anything electronic (computer, stereo, iPod, TV)
- privileges (use of car, freedom to stay up later, boat, family property)
- what a parent may provide (car insurance, vacation, a home, gas money, allowance)

An appropriate consequence might also be a work project or duty.

The reason for establishing consequences is to keep your children from behaving a particular way, not simply to punish them for wrongdoing. Focus on correction more than justice, direction more than punishment, and guidance more than retribution. The reason for establishing a belief system is to determine the path your children should take and to keep them from going somewhere they really don't want to go, not just to figure out what punishment they should get for doing something wrong or unacceptable.

Begin by prioritizing your beliefs and rules. Match the greatest consequences to the highest priorities. If you consider academics to be the highest priority for your child, then tie the toughest consequence to poor academic performance. For instance, if your children love being on the computer more than anything in the world, take away their computer privileges for a couple of weeks as the consequence for not passing all their classes.

Personally, my big issues with kids are respect, obedience, and honesty. The toughest consequences would be attached to any violation of those. I would focus on behaviors like drug or alcohol use, driving under the influence, and physical issues, like violence or sexual promiscuity.

Allow me to take the areas I listed earlier and set some rules to each with corresponding consequences to give you an idea of what a belief system might look like. But let me encourage you to come up with your own rules and consequences to fit your children, their ages, and their situations, all based on what you desire to accomplish with your family.

Academic
- Belief: Our children should be able to pass all their classes throughout their high school years.
- Rule: There will be no failing grades in school.
- Consequence: No computer time at home other than for homework until all grades are passing grades.

Spiritual
- Belief: Our children will attend church or some other resource for spiritual input.
- Rule: Our children will attend church once a week.
- Consequence: Loss of Friday night out.

Social
- Belief: Nothing good happens after midnight.
- Rule: Curfew is midnight on weekends.
- Consequence: Loss of allowance for two weeks.

Behavioral
- Belief: Each family member should be treated with respect.
- Rule: All family members will treat each other with the utmost respect.
- Consequence: First offense: grounding for one week, which includes the loss of all privileges except attendance at school and job responsibilities. Repeated offenses: grounding for two-week periods with loss of the car and loss of allowance. If this grounding is not effective, the car will be sold or computer given away.

Character

- Belief: Family members should strive to improve their character.

- Rule: Each family member will have breakfast with either Mom or Dad once a week to talk about life issues and discuss the future. In addition, one week every summer will be devoted to working on a mission project somewhere.

- Consequence: No Saturday night out.

Medical

- Belief: Every family member should follow any medical advice.

- Rule: Everyone in this family will take all prescribed medicine.

- Consequence: iPods, TV, and other electrical devices in the house will be left off.

Possessions

- Belief: Bedrooms should be cleaned regularly.

- Rule: A messy room is okay throughout the week, but it must be cleaned every other week. Cleaning includes dusting, vacuuming, and picking up anything that doesn't belong on the floor.

- Consequence: Loss of allowance for one week.

Entertainment

- Belief: R-rated movies should not be seen in our home.

- Rule: R-rated movies will be allowed only if approved by Mom. These must be given to her a few days in advance.

- Consequence: Loss of TV for a month and the poking out of one eye (just kidding).

Responsibilities
- Belief: Teenagers should be able to do their own laundry.
- Rule: Each person will be responsible to wash, fold, and put away his or her laundry each week.
- Consequence: Soiled clothes will be confiscated and can be purchased back from Mom.

Privileges
- Belief: Family members should know where everyone is at all times.
- Rule: When there is a change of plans, use the cell phone we've provided to call and let us know of the change.
- Consequence: A four-hour work project.

Family
- Belief: The family should have at least one night a week together.
- Rule: The entire family will eat dinner together and enjoy an activity every Monday night.
- Consequence: No inheritance (also a joke).

I've learned a few invaluable lessons about rules through the years. One is to use humor. Humor will always make a pill a little easier to swallow. Most young people would feel a little constrained by this belief system, but with a little humor, they will tend to respond more positively.

Also, rules without relationship cause rebellion. If you don't have relationships with your children, they will view rules as herd management or a way to keep you from getting frustrated. If you don't have a relationship, let your children know of your desire to build one and add to the relational side of the belief system extra time together, a trip somewhere, or a weekly parent/child time together.

I've found that young people want rules. They want to know what is expected and what is not. Kids feel freer when they know where the boundaries are. They want to know what's important to Mom and

Dad and when they get to make their own choices. We require all the families at Heartlight to put together a belief system for their homes before their children return. I often laugh because the children usually come up with harder rules than the parents do! The children who have been in our program understand that a set of expectations and clearly defined directives helps relationships flourish. Deep down, the kids desire to have a relationship with Mom and Dad.

Wouldn't that be nice? To have a child who really wants a relationship with you? By establishing a belief system, you help make that possible, especially if you've lost that relationship. And once your system is in place, you can allow some things to happen that we discussed in the first half of the book—allowing pain to enter the picture and helping your child begin to understand the concept of consequences.

You are now allowing your children the opportunity to flourish as they have the freedom to fail. Sure, their clothes are going to be all pink a couple times as they learn to do their own laundry, but as they accept responsibility and take on some new rules, they will learn that it's time to grow up. Not an easy thing for a Mom or Dad to watch. But in time, the belief system you have crafted for your family will yield great benefits.

CHAPTER ELEVEN

SETTING BOUNDARIES

Jan and I had just returned home. The moment we walked into our home I felt like one of the three bears who knew someone had eaten his food, slept in his bed, and sat in his chair. I had a sneaking suspicion that our son, Adam, had been up to something at our home while we had been away on vacation.

Just the weekend before we had visited Texas Tech with Adam to look at the school. After spending some time there he decided that this wasn't the place because he didn't see enough trees, and he saw too much alcohol. I supported his decision and was impressed that he based his choice on a couple of good principles. (Yes, I was born in Midland, Texas, where people dream of tall pines and fall foliage!)

When we returned, Jan and I got ready to go on a little vacation by ourselves. We let him know that while we were gone, we would trust him. No one was to come over or spend the night, and he was to take care of the house, dogs, and any problems that came up. We felt confident that he could handle the responsibilities. Shoot, he'd better be able to—he was going off to college in a few months!

Upon our return, I walked in the door and noticed dirt was on the floor, food was gone, beds were messed up, and our bathroom tub had been used. A feeling of uneasiness ruined the relaxing effects of our vacation. I asked Adam if anything happened while we were gone. He said, "Nope, nothing happened. I'll get everything cleaned up."

Later that night, I went up to his room and asked again, "You sure nothing happened here while we were gone?" "I'm sure, Dad," he replied. I thought to myself, *I know I was born at night, but I wasn't born last night.* I've had kids lying to me almost all my life, and my son suddenly showed all the symptoms of one who was lying through his teeth. I knew something had gone on, and I was now on a mission to find out what it was.

The next day I decided to mow the lawn. Riding the mower around gives me time to think. I came upon a few dozen beer bottle caps, and immediately thought I should call the local airline for dumping their waste out of their plane because it landed in my yard. When Adam got home from school, I told him about the airline dumping these beer bottle caps and that I was going to file a complaint.

He could no longer hide his guilt and embarrassment. "Dad, something did go on while you guys were gone." I asked, "Really...what?" He replied, "I wish I could tell you, but I don't remember." He had been a little too tanked to know all that had gone on. And while he was blitzed, some other guys took advantage of the situation.

Beer, wine coolers, cigars, girls, and partying filled the house and emptied my confidence that Adam had developed some good principles to live by. He apologized, and we grounded him for a while. Not much else you can do to an 18-year-old who's headed off to college.

You know what bothered me the most? It wasn't the fact that he violated our rules of the house, nor was it the experimentation with beer, wine coolers, and cigars. It wasn't that he went against what we asked. It wasn't that he didn't fulfill the responsibilities we had given him. It wasn't that others had snuck around behind our backs. And it wasn't that an airliner had dumped beer bottle caps into our yard.

What bothered me most was the personal violation I felt. He walked all over our boundaries and tried to cover his actions. His disrespect made his apologies a little hollow.

It's All About Respect

The belief system we discussed in the last chapter is vital to getting your house in order. It's a step in the right direction. This chapter is about you and your need to set boundaries for yourself, for your home, and for your family. These boundaries are not about how to run your home; they are about respecting you as the parent.

As you read in the last chapter, I believe respect is the main issue in any home. If children don't develop the character trait of respect, a belief system will not bring transformation. Without a sense of respect for others they will not create meaningful relationships or succeed in life. By creating boundaries for your own life and home, and by teaching your children to respect those boundaries, you can restore or enhance your relationship with your children.

I know of a couple that moved hundreds of miles away from their grown kids so they could live with boundaries in their lives. They gave up their friends, their church, and their beautiful home and moved far away to start over. They just couldn't get their grown kids to respect their boundaries, so they went looking for a place where they would be respected.

A little disrespect from your children can threaten to ruin your life and tempt you to give it all up to move to a place where people respect you and your boundaries.

Perhaps you know those feelings because you have been violated by your teen. Do any of these feel familiar?

You've been walked on.

You've been forced to do some things you don't want to do.

You've been treated shamefully by your kids.

Your life has revolved around them for years.

You have no life, no outlet, and you're going crazy.

Your kids dump on you, take it out on you, and beat you up verbally.

Your teen has gotten physically violent.

You're at their beck and call by default rather than by plan.

You have been emotionally and psychologically violated.

You've been lied to, deceived, manipulated, and shouted at.

Sounds like the making of a good country song doesn't it? But these feelings are real, and they can make you want to run, regardless of how good your belief system looks on paper. Any belief system is only as powerful as the person behind it. It is simply a tool parents can use to guide their children.

It *Is* About You

My encouragement to you as a parent is to set some boundaries that are about you. Choose boundaries that will help you be the person God has called you to be in your family.

This is the place in this book where it *is* about you. It's about your ability to lead your family to a place that is respectful, orderly, and relational. And if you're going to steer this herd, you've got to take care of *you!*

The power and authority you possess will determine the strength of the rules, beliefs, and requirements you have set within your home. Without your child's respect, rules mean nothing. Your children must learn to respect you in your decisions, whether they agree or not. Respect you as a person. Respect your limits. And respect your boundaries, regardless of how absurd they think they might be.

What Are Boundaries?

Boundaries are those parameters or fences that define our own space. They describe what is ours and what is not. They may include locks on doors, words that reflect our personal desires, or rules, standards, and principles by which we choose to live. They may make distinctions between what is off limits and what is okay for you.

Boundaries allow you to establish your priorities. They let the fruit of self-control grow in your life. They give you a sense of backbone and a sense of confidence to not let everyone walk on you. They define who you are and who you are not.

Henry Cloud and John Townsend, in their book *Boundaries*, offer this clarification: "Boundaries define us. They define what is me and what is not me. A boundary shows me where I end and someone else begins, leading me to a sense of ownership."[1]

The Parenting Shift

As our children grow, we must shift our style of parenting. We transition from provision, which is appropriate for children in their elementary school years, to preparation, which helps young people become mature and responsible. Sadly, rather than strategically planning this transition, most parents wait until conflict forces the shift.

The transition works best when it is clearly defined. It should send a message to your children that says, "The way we have operated is changing, and there are new expectations, new boundaries, and new responsibilities."

The Jewish community celebrates this transition with a bat mitzvah for girls and a bar mitzvah for boys. In these formal ceremonies, the family and community recognize that children are entering adulthood. The events recognize the onset of this important transition.

These ceremonies are marked by celebration, merriment, gift giving, blessings, and honoring of the teen. Unfortunately, for many Gentile families, this transition is a time of strife, confusion, and distress. But it doesn't have to be that way.

So let me make a suggestion. When your children reach adolescence—I would choose age 13—create a special time when you formally recognize the transition to more responsibility and maturity. Mark a change in the way you relate to them—no longer as children but now as young adults. If you don't make the shift proactively, you will more than likely be forced to make the shift at a point of conflict.

What will you shift?

- the way you teach, moving from lecture to discussion
- the way you mentor, from doing it for them to allowing them to do it for themselves (even if they may fail)
- from a mind-set of providing to a mind-set of preparing

- from being in control to allowing them being in control
- the way you discipline, no longer punishing but moving them in a direction

The parenting style that worked for you in elementary school won't work during the middle school and junior high years. And what worked for you in the middle school and junior high years won't work for you in the high school years. And what worked in high school won't work in the college years. As your kids grow, they will think your previous parenting style is childish. Too many parents don't make this shift in how they parent as their children grow, and they end up provoking their children, who become frustrated, irritated, and aggravated.

If your children still...

- dig through your purse
- walk into your bathroom unannounced
- don't clean up after themselves
- don't act as if anyone else lives in the house
- yell and scream at you
- demand you do things the way you always have
- are lazy and won't work around the house
- emotionally dump on you whenever there is a problem
- make demeaning and arrogant comments to you and about you
- and require you to be their servants,

you have a problem. And it's not a problem with the child. It's a problem with boundaries.

Clearly, the shift hasn't happened in your children's minds. Perhaps it hasn't happened in yours. And it won't until you make it happen or are forced to do so because of a crisis.

Responses to Boundaries

If you present new boundaries and new responsibilities with celebration and festivity, your kids will receive those boundaries as gifts. But when these new boundaries and responsibilities are given in conflict and crisis, kids will feel restricted and limited at a time when they believe they should be given more freedom and greater territory.

So, of course, the most effective way to handle the shift is to build a tradition in your family that marks the age of 13 as the beginning of adulthood. If your kids are under the age of 13, now would be a good time to build this concept into your belief system so your family can look forward to that time and celebrate it.

But if your child is older, and you have missed the opportunity to acknowledge this transition, then I suggest you look for a time to make this transition official. Look to your child's next birthday, and allow that birthday to usher in a new way of thinking and new expectations.

Leslie

When Leslie came to us, she was spinning out of control. She was drinking, partying, skipping school, engulfed sexually with a young man, hating everything, and out to prove her dislike for the world and everyone in it. She wasn't exactly the most enjoyable teen to be around.

She openly expressed her hatred of her dad. She made it clear that she thought he was a wimp, that he always treated her like a little girl, and that he needed her a lot more than she needed him. She felt about the same way about her mom. She felt as if her mother was always smothering her, never giving her any space to breathe, and always wanting to "be there for her." And she felt like Mom also treated her as if she were a little kid.

Leslie's dad told me, "I gave up all hope of ever having a relationship with her. For a few years our eyes rarely made contact except to exchange angry glances. She is a confused little girl who shared nothing but hatred for me. I once told her I never wanted to see her again." Her mom shared that her little princess had turned into a witch, and the one whom she had loved so dearly, she now couldn't stand to be around.

As Leslie's mom and dad poured out their hearts, I thought to myself, *What a mess*. I even questioned at the time if I really wanted to dive in and try to help them get out of this whirlpool of losing a teen. I really didn't see much hope. I saw a father who had given up on his daughter, a mother who was broken and feeling lost, and a daughter who didn't care about anyone or anything, including her parents.

After months of conversations, counseling, observations, and cups of coffee, I finally realized why this family didn't have any boundaries. It was the result of the position in which they had placed Leslie. They were idolizing their daughter, and setting boundaries around someone you idolize is almost impossible.

Leslie was their pride and joy. They lived their life for her and worshipped her. No child could live up to those expectations. Leslie's behavior was designed to prove to them that she was not perfect and to send the message that she wasn't going to allow them to put her on a pedestal.

This young lady was actually establishing some of her own boundaries. And though she was not doing it in the best of ways, her intent was to create her own identity and break away from a fantasy her parents had created.

Mom and Dad needed to let her go, to let her grow up, to start acting like a mom and dad. Leslie needed to become a daughter with boundaries and stop being a goddess who could do no wrong.

My first task was to help Leslie's parents take her off the pedestal. The second task was to help them put some boundaries into place that would define and protect the positions that each was to have in their family. Leslie's dad later stated, "You helped us to grow as parents and to recognize and embrace the hurt, frustrated, and angry adolescents that *we* still were. That not only helped us but also helped Leslie through our process of self-discovery."

Leslie's mom shared that she began to realize that she needed to take her children off the pedestal and begin to set some boundaries within the home so that everyone could flourish and grow. Leslie had to learn to be loved in a new way. Boundaries helped get their situation under control.

Candice

Candice was a 14-year-old girl who had been coddled for most of her life. She had been pampered mostly by her mother, who had never established boundaries because of the guilt she felt from a divorce when Candice was five and because of her own need to have a relationship with her daughter. That relationship was more of a peer friendship than a parenting relationship. Candice was out of control. Her mother knew it but felt helpless.

Candice was one of those girls I really didn't like when I first met her. She would break things and not show any remorse. Anything she did wrong, she believed, was someone else's fault. She'd walk in the bathroom when it was occupied. She'd yell and scream at anyone at any time for any reason. Her temperament was volatile, and people went out of their way to avoid her. She borrowed other girls' things without asking and didn't think anything was wrong. When confronted about the way she treated someone, she would immediately say she was sorry, but she would do it in such a way that if anyone wanted to go any further, she would say, "I said I'm sorry…what else do you want me to do?"

I decided the best way to approach her was to put just one boundary before her. And it was this: I expected her to act her age, and I would treat her the same. Most of the time, I felt like I was correcting a 5-year-old who had a mouth of a 25-year-old, and that needed to change.

Not surprisingly, her response to my suggestion was horrible because my approach limited her ability to act the way she did. She not only rejected limits, restrictions, and boundaries, she hated them. The first time I confronted her, she walked into her house and shaved her head. About an hour later she came out to show me what she had done and how she left just one square inch of a six-inch length of hair on the front of her head. She was out to get me and to express her frustration.

She was telling me I had just violated one of her boundaries, and she was going to show me that I shouldn't do that.

I told her that she looked good with no hair—not a comment she wanted to hear. And just before she stormed off, I told her that she was now getting a taste of how it felt to have her boundaries crossed. It just made her even more mad, and her anger increased over the next few months.

My heart aches when I see young people stick to their guns and hold onto their lifestyle because they fear impending change. Candice's stubbornness kept her in a painful place for a long time. But her anger also gave us a flicker of hope. Remember, anger is like a dashboard warning light. And the signal she gave off when she was mad was that we were getting closer to the issues she was harboring.

We had one confrontation after another, one fight after another, one long emotional draining interaction after another. But as we taught, fought, confronted, loved on, and spent time with Candice—and as the other kids at Heartlight shared with her in group therapy meetings what they saw in her—she began to realize she was separated and isolated from relationships because of her unwillingness to respect other people's boundaries. She eventually began to see how she really was. And because what she saw was so ugly, she ran the other direction. Her response was not perfect, but she was at least willing to change for the better.

My purpose in sharing Candice's story is to help prepare you for a struggle when you first place boundaries on kids. It's like putting a bridle on a horse that has been running free for years. Be prepared for the response and possible reaction. The fight is usually long and hard. The earlier you can begin the process, the better.

Do Boundaries Always Work?

People often ask if this "boundary thing" always works. The answer is no. Some kids just won't accept the boundaries. Young men usually want independence and often react against restrictions.

Young ladies, on the other hand, want intimacy, which is usually found through relationships developed in social circles. They are so relational that when you begin to restrict social gatherings and social interactions, you might get a pretty strong reaction. For example, a girl may fly off the handle if she is kept from going to the prom because of inappropriate behavior.

When boundaries are determined early, children will get used to the authority of parents. They will learn the ropes of relationships and discover the fences of appropriate behavior. On the other hand, imposing new boundaries on older teens is a disaster waiting to happen. It's like allowing a boy to drive at age 16 and then taking away his license until he's 17. Your teens will probably respond a little more intensely if they've already tasted freedom.

So what's the point? First, if you have the chance, set the boundaries early. And if you are just now trying to set those boundaries with your older teens, expect a fight as you implement your boundaries. That doesn't mean your boundaries are wrong, it just means you have to be prepared. Remember, kids' reactions to boundaries are not indicators of their appropriateness.

Quite honestly, I've seen some horses I just can't break. They're too old, have too many habits, and have gotten too used to not being handled. Unless you're a horse whisperer with a ton of experience, chances are the older ones won't accept a bridle.

At that point, a parent has a choice to make. You can allow your child to remain at home, where you will have to batten down the hatches and prepare for stormy weather. Or you can send your child to a place like Heartlight, where kids get over their issues with boundaries.

Some kids who never responded to boundaries at home eventually learn those boundaries in the workplace, in a college setting, or in a marriage. Some even learn boundaries for themselves when they have their own children. Unfortunately, they will more than likely be fired a few times, get kicked out of school, or even lose a marriage in the process of learning those boundaries.

Respecting Your Boundaries

As I wrote earlier, a belief system helps get your house in order. And setting boundaries helps you get your belief system in order. Setting boundaries for yourself tells your children, "This is who I am," "This is who we are," and "This is what our home will be like."

Nothing is wrong with letting people know what you want and asking them to respect your wishes. It's okay to ask them to knock on the door, not to take things without asking, not to drive your car, to stay out of your room and bathroom, and not to borrow your clothes. It's okay to have some of your own space.

You are defining what you want and who you are. You are choosing to fence, protect, and put limits around yourself and your home and family. You are clarifying those things that are valuable to you.

Establishing boundaries empowers you. And it also allows a child to make decisions and choose consequences in volatile situations. You set the boundaries and rules, and your child decides if he or she is going to break those rules, thus choosing the consequences.

As your child moves into the teen years, you can put to rest some old habits, routines, and practices that have become a way of life. Slamming doors. Watching cartoons on Saturday morning. Sleeping late on certain mornings. The way you interact as a family. Be willing to set boundaries that put a stop to certain things that are no longer acceptable.

When we first started Heartlight, our family lived in one room for two and a half years. It was so cramped, each night we had to rotate from the bed to the sofa to the floor (we only had one bed that slept two). My son was in third grade, my daughter in seventh. One morning my daughter, Melissa, was taking her frustrations out on my wife, Jan. To make a long story short, I intervened when the verbal intensity got out of hand and Melissa was being disrespectful.

I walked into the bathroom where they were verbally duking it out, put my finger on my daughter, and looked her straight in the eye with the intensity of a wrestler staring down his opponent. I said, "You will not treat my wife like this anymore. Understand?" She got the message loud and clear. I established a boundary and helped my wife remember she was worth fighting for.

You can set boundaries around your time. Driving kids to school, sports events, church events, and social activities takes time. Being involved in your kids' schoolwork takes time. Shopping, cleaning, fixing, helping…no wonder many parents struggle when their kids go off to college; they don't have a life of their own.

Sometimes it's okay to say, "I can't do that," and allow your child to go it alone. It's okay to have some personal time. And it's okay to not do something because you'd rather do something else. Your behavior teaches kids to do the same. Your mentoring in this area will show them the value of boundaries and help them understand the need to set them in their own life as well.

Respect Their Boundaries

As your teens see your boundaries, they will learn to develop boundaries for themselves. However, because of their selfish nature, their quest for independence, and their desire to make decisions on their own, they won't want you to meddle in their personal affairs. But as a parent, you will still need to determine what is appropriate and not appropriate.

The older teens get, the more decisions they should be making for themselves. Children will set some boundaries for themselves that you must respect, but you will set some boundaries for them that they must respect. And generally, if your kids' boundaries violate your family's beliefs and rules, you would probably be right to violate their boundaries.

For example, as controversial as this may be, I think parents have the right to inspect children's journals, review cell phone bills, look at e-mails, and check the Internet viewing history. I would also encourage parents to put recorders on computers that map and log communication on the computer. If your child is doing something illegal, participating in something that is potentially detrimental or harmful, or doing anything that gives you a feeling that something isn't right, I would encourage looking at anything and everything.

Of course, tell your kids beforehand that you will be doing this. Tell them about the software on the computer that will tell you every place they've been and everything they've typed. Tell them you will respect their privacy, but you will also do whatever is necessary to determine if they are participating in something that is unacceptable in your home.

The Stage Is Set

I spoke at a church not too long ago that had one of the most fantastic youth buildings I have ever seen. It cost $4 million, and was designed to create an environment that was attractive to teens, helped them feel valuable, and created new opportunities for ministry. I was in awe as I saw how much this church valued its youth.

The room I was to speak in was gorgeous. The lighting was fantastic, the sound system was crisp, the air conditioning was perfect. The setup was superb, and all the planning had brought a large crowd. Anticipation filled the air.

Then I walked up to speak.

When I got up front, I noticed (as did everyone else) that the lighting was aimed somewhere other than where I was standing. About five minutes after I began, the microphone went dead. A little later, the air conditioning—which was on an electrical timer—quit.

What was a perfect setting by all appearances had quickly become dim, hot, and silent. Before long I was standing in the dark, sweating and yelling (and even then, not everyone could hear me). Something so well-intentioned, so well planned, and so well set up, had become a disaster in just an hour and a half. And the reason it did was evident. The person in charge thought everything was okay, so he left.

That evening reinforced for me some important lessons. First, never assume everything will remain okay. As you put together a belief system for your home and set boundaries, remain engaged with your family, and don't assume that the system will take care of itself. As time passes, you'll discover areas that need more attention.

Second, regardless of how beautiful your system may appear, it will never run on its own. It takes your *constant* involvement. When God told Joshua to cross the Jordan River and enter the promised land, He added, "I will never leave you nor forsake you."

This same message must be communicated to our teens, especially during times of struggle and difficulty. A system won't fix anything on its own. A system *within the context of relationships* will lead a child into the right relationships with those who love him.

Once the stage is set, don't leave. Stay engaged. You never know when an airline is going to dump its beer bottle caps in your yard.

CHAPTER TWELVE

ALLOWING YOUR CHILD TO BE IN CONTROL

G od has called you to an incredibly challenging role as a parent. But your hope and confidence will continue to grow as you discover and apply principles that can help you get your children where they need to be.

In all the challenges you face as a parent, never lose perspective on the primary role God has called you to as a mom or dad: to lead your children from total dependency at birth to independency at the end of their teenage years.

As we have seen, your parenting style will shift as your child ages. These shifts must occur in sync with your child's maturation process; otherwise, your children will end up frustrated because they either want more freedom or aren't prepared to handle life's challenges.

The various stages of parenting are simple. Knowing when to move from one stage to the next is much more difficult. And poor timing can lead to rebellion, frustration, and confusion.

The Four *P*s of Parenting

In this chapter, my intent is not to discuss the developmental stages of children. Rather, I'll outline a progression in your parenting style that can be immensely valuable as you lead your child to independence. The stages overlap, but clarifying parents' changing roles can be helpful.

Stage One: Pleasing Your Child

From a child's birth through the preschool years, the parents' primary role is to please their child. They do that by offering relief from pain, unhappiness, and sickness.

Nobody enjoys a baby who is colicky or fussy. And everyone loves a baby who sleeps through the night. A "good baby is a happy baby." If a baby cries, parents do whatever they can to quiet him. If he is fussy, parents try to figure out what is bothering him and then do whatever they can to soothe him. No wonder these little kids feel like the center of a parent's world. They are!

In this first stage of pleasing your child, you have total control.

Stage Two: Protecting Your Child

When our children are in their elementary years, they would probably accidentally kill themselves if we weren't around to protect them. Keeping them from dangerous and inappropriate activities and influences becomes one of the major focuses of parenting at this stage.

When boys' thrill for adventure exceed their understanding of safety, parents worry about them getting hurt in sports, on the playground, on their bikes, climbing trees, or just clowning around. Parents also don't want their children to suffer rejection or to be exposed to anything violent, sexual, or immoral.

In this second stage, we want to maintain control.

Stage Three: Providing for Your Child

The third stage of parenting is providing for your child. This stage usually begins in the junior high years.

We begin to give our junior high children experiences, possessions, and opportunities that are far greater than what we gave them in the elementary years. We allow them to spread their wings a little, and we begin to expose them to the world outside the home.

At this stage, others begin to coach, teach, instruct, train, tutor, mentor, and educate our kids. Our children begin to get serious about sports, music, and academics.

They also begin to go to youth group, Bible studies, mission trips, ski trips, overnighters, slumber parties, and organized sports and school activities. They may take a school trip to Washington D.C., and we begin to trust others to take care of our children.

In this third stage, we realize we can lose control.

Stage Four: Preparing Your Child

The fourth stage of parenting usually begins during the high school years, when a child is being prepared to move out of the nest and into a new life outside of the home.

This is when you begin to hand over control. And it's the stage when we feel like we're losing control. And the truth of the matter is that we are. You give control of your children's lives to them so they can function independently by the time they leave home.

Good Intentions Aren't Enough

I am constantly asked by puzzled parents, "How can something so well-intentioned go so wrong?"

It's a good question. And easy to answer when you understand free choice. But the real issue for most of these parents is whether they have been led astray or have done something wrong without knowing it.

Without question I believe some parents have indeed been led astray and have, as a result, messed up. When parents are desperate for answers for their children, they'll sometimes listen to anything.

Some well-meaning parents get stuck at a certain stage of parenting because they don't know what lies ahead, or they don't recognize the need to move to the next stage, or they don't understand that decisions and habits developed during one stage must shift when moving to the next. For example, if parents don't shift out of always pleasing their children, they'll be in trouble when their kids get to seventh and eighth grade. And if parents never move out of their protective stage and let their kids taste the outside world, the situation will be devastating on both kids and parents by the high school years. And if parents never prepare kids during the high school years for the world ahead, disorder and confusion will surround kids in their college years.

Sometimes provision in one stage becomes enabling in another, even with the best of intentions.

Furthermore, if parents don't let go of the major emphasis of each stage of parenting by the time kids are in high school, they will create a real mess. If parents still try to please at all cost, strive to protect in every circumstance, and struggle to make sure they constantly provide all their children's needs, they will create a muddled, mixed up, and chaotic atmosphere. Their children will act out because they feel insecure and unprepared to enter the world, or they will be frustrated that they can't get out of the world they have outgrown.

A Perspective on Homeschooling

Some Christian teens pay a great price for parents who have well-intentioned hearts to protect their children. This often comes with homeschooling, setting high standards, placing tight boundaries, and preventing exposure to anything that challenges the family's beliefs. Believe me; I am not against homeschooling, standards, boundaries, and protection. But I also believe we must prepare our children to function well in the world in which they will eventually live. They are not to be *of* the world, but they need to know how to live in it.

Our residential counseling program works with kids who are struggling. These kids are no different from yours and mine who have been raised in Christian homes. Our ministry is mainly directed at Christian families. And many of the kids who have come to us have been homeschooled, raised with the highest standards, and kept from anything remotely non-Christian. But what I hear most from these kids is this: "My parents are overprotective," "They have high standards that no one can live up to," and "They won't let me do anything."

Time and time again these kids tell me that the people they associate with in their homeschool programs are socially isolated and inept. Do I believe that only dorky kids are homeschooled? No. But I do believe that the lack of social interaction for some prevents them from learning to function well socially.

Many times I've seen homeschooled kids really struggle when they are sent off to public school. The guys are ridiculed and the girls are exploited. And when parents hear what is happening, they are even more convinced they need to homeschool their children. They believe their children's experience only justifies homeschooling in the first place. They don't realize their choice to homeschool may have caused the problems.

Here's my point. Who pays the price for Mom and Dad's well-intentioned choice? The child. A child will either retreat, run, or rebel. Can you blame kids for those responses when they are thrust into a world they haven't been prepared to live in? No wonder they isolate. No wonder they run away. And no wonder they rebel.

People are usually shocked when I tell them that one of the largest groups of kids at Heartlight includes those who have been homeschooled beyond the eighth grade. Again, I'm not against homeschooling or protecting our kids. But if your protocol of schooling does not include the opportunity for your child to make decisions, formulate choices, and experience small bits of social hurt, conflict, and rejection, you are just postponing the inevitable. And the longer you wait, the harder it will hit your child, and the pain can be more than many adults can handle.

I'm not just talking about socialization issues. I'm including developmental opportunities and peer integration needs. Your children need to learn to make choices.

You don't want your son confronted with making a decision for the first time when he is in the ninth grade and deciding whether he's going to smoke pot with his new friends because he wants so desperately to fit in. And you don't want your beautiful daughter having to make her first decision about sexual activity when a hormone-laden young man is trying to convince her that he can help her fit in socially.

If your children are going to be homeschooled, they need opportunities to mix with those who disagree with them or are different from them, and they need to make decisions in that context. Small bits of social hurt, conflict, and rejection create opportunities for parents to impart wisdom in the midst of the pain.

Many parents ask me how long a child should be homeschooled. My answer is this: As long as you want. But sometime during the elementary years, I would encourage you to begin to allow your child to experience a little of what you have protected him or her from. If you do, your child will be better prepared to enter their social world.

Remember, your children have been created for relationships. With you, yes. With God, absolutely. But they also need relationships with others their own age. You will instill a sense of value in your children, but that value will be authenticated by their peers. The acceptance by peers will help move your children into the current of society and prevent them from fearing a world they have been created to be in.

This process of allowing your homeschooled children to interact with and experience some of the things you have protected them from needs to continue in the seventh- and eighth-grade years. These years are when kids begin to practice what they have learned—outside the protective shield of homeschooling.

Mark Twain, in *A Tramp Abroad,* said it best: "The most permanent lessons in morals are those which come, not of booky teaching, but of experience."[1] If you haven't made this transition of letting your children experience some of the world so they can better prepare for what is to come, I want you to know it's never too late. But you may need to create a strategy that will help your children catch up but won't overwhelm them. Talk with your child so that he or she knows and understands the process.

Let me assure you, exposure to the world makes for some pretty interesting discussions. And it can reinforce kids' desire for a relationship with Christ as they grasp His love for the world and see the world's need.

Transferring Control

If your child has been overly controlled, it's time to shift some of that control over to your child. You may be overly controlling because your family lacks boundaries and a belief system that help kids make decisions. As a result, your child may be immature and irresponsible.

When I make this statement to parents, they often reply, "My daughter is immature and irresponsible, and you want me to transfer control over to her? You've got to be kidding!"

If that's what you are thinking, let me give you some important perspective. First, he who is faithful in little is faithful in much. If you wait to transfer control until your children are "successful" (displaying maturity and responsibility), you will thwart their maturation. You give a little because that's what your child needs, not because your child deserves it. If you gave your children what they really deserved, they'd probably never be able to leave home! Transferring control before you and your teen are struggling is always best.

Overly controlled children are raised by loving parents who try to protect their children from making mistakes, try to keep them from being exposed to harmful influences outside the home, or try to keep them from failure. Dr. Henry Cloud states, "Over controlled children are subject to dependency, enmeshment conflicts, and difficulty setting and keeping firm boundaries. They also have problems taking risks and being creative."[2]

Anna

I was teaching a seminar in Richmond, Virginia, when a young mother shared with me during lunch that she thought her 14-year-old daughter, Anna, had a reactive detachment disorder. She shared that her daughter was very disrespectful at home, always rolling her eyes, cussing, yelling, and screaming at her parents. She was verbally aggressive, attacking, and insolent.

When I asked more about Anna, I found that she had been adopted from Korea when she was eight and was now being homeschooled after two years in the public school. The home intentionally had no TV, no Internet access, no privileges to talk on the phone, and no opportunity to play any type of sports.

The parents allowed Anna to go to church and a small group that met once a week. They also boarded a horse for Anna and her brother, who was a year younger, and allowed each of the kids to have their own dog. Other people at church loved Anna and thought she was a wonderful young lady. The small group leader loved having Anna in her group.

After an hour and a half of a rather inquisitive discussion, Anna's mom finally asked me, "Do you think this is about us?" I hesitated to answer. I don't have a problem sharing the truth with parents about what I have observed, but I was moved by this lady's passion for her daughter, and I didn't want her to give up doing good things for Anna.

But before I could answer, she said, "It is about us, isn't it?" I said, "Yeah, it sounds like it." We talked for a couple of hours about why Anna does what she does, the impact of her adoption, issues surrounding the losses Anna has experienced, and what was driving Anna's issue with control. I eventually agreed with Anna's mom that Anna had "reactive detachment."

But I saw a problem with that conclusion. Anna was only reactive to her parents—and they seemed to be the only people she was detached from. This "disorder" is usually not selective. I finally concluded that her reactive detachment really wasn't that. It was rebellion.

Because of Anna's mother's love for horses and dogs, I used this analogy. I had taken in an orphan dog named Copper (not that I intended to compare her daughter to a dog) and put it in the kennel with my other two golden retrievers. When we first took him in, Copper was a great dog. After a couple of weeks, a couple of the kids at Heartlight came over to play with the three dogs. They told me that Copper was jumping on them, playfully bit one of the girls, wouldn't listen, was constantly barking, and was extremely hyper.

My great idea to take in an orphan dog had turned it into a bad dog. The problem wasn't with the dog. The problem was that I put him in the kennel. Copper was a young dog that needed to run. He needed more time outside the kennel. He didn't need more training. He needed to be given the opportunity to be a dog. I could discipline him all I want, but all I really needed to do was to change my plan and accommodate his needs.

I complimented Anna's mom for wanting to protect her child from the things of the world. Kids need that. But what Anna needed now, without even knowing it, was to be given some room to "run," or she would continue to rebel. Too much restriction and control would squeeze anyone to rebel. Anna was really responding normally (even though she displayed it inappropriately) to a level of control that was once appropriate but now was most inappropriate.

Randy

When Randy came to live with us, he was 16 years old. His parents had just gone through a horrendously nasty divorce. They were consumed with the fight, and didn't pay much attention to their son. As a result, Randy started to make his own decisions, do his own thing, and live without any guidance from Mom or Dad. He tried his best to keep things together and function as best he could in two worlds—a home that was falling apart and an everyday life that was pulling him in every direction. After Randy spent two years functioning pretty much on his own, his mother tried to reengage with him, telling him what to do and placing restrictions on him that challenged his acquired survivor skills and his new way of living without rules, directives, or boundaries.

Randy was resilient and had weathered his parents' storm in a way that was amazing for a 16-year-old. But along the way he failed a few times…and because Mom couldn't reestablish control, she sent him to live with us.

Randy's sense of humor was attractive and contagious. His people skills were amazing. And his compassion for everyone who struggled was touching. He was a salesman at heart (he could sell snow to Eskimos) and had learned to manipulate his world to survive. These were great skills for someone who lived on his own. But not so great when Mom was trying to get her house in order.

Randy told me he thought the real problem was that he was just "too old for his age." He said that if he were just a couple of years older, everything he was doing that got him sent to us would really be okay. I couldn't have agreed with him more.

Trying to control children who have already been in control is like using the same old rules with a college kid who has come home after living on his own. It's just never the same. I see this happen quite a bit in various situations: in cases of divorce, when a parent dies and the remaining parent remarries and tries to set up a new home, or when kids are exposed to something or experience something that is so out of the ordinary that they grow up too fast and are forced to take control of their lives.

In cases like these—and like Randy's—the question is not whether you will give them control. The question is how kids who already have control function in a home where they don't get to make all the decisions. Randy wasn't *acting* like he was too big for his britches. He *was* too big for his britches.

Todd

Some kids are like Todd, who at 16 would rather be at home spending time in isolation than being with friends (he has none), working, going to school, or participating in other social activities. I met with Todd's dad following a speaking engagement in Tampa, Florida. He called his son the basement hermit and said Todd had no social skills and preferred to be watching TV, surfing the Internet, playing a video game, watching movies, or doing homework—all activities that involve no one and require no interaction. Todd's mom said that the only control he has in his life is the remote and the key on his computer.

Todd, as a normal kid in elementary school, was allowed to spend inordinate amounts of time on the computer either surfing the Internet or playing games. Today he can find just about any information he wants and can score high on most games.

The problem created by this nonsocial pastime, however, is that he didn't learn the social skills he needed for his seventh- and eighth-grade years. As a result, those years were socially devastating for him. So now he isolates himself out of fear, and justifiably so. Beneath the fear, Todd has a strong desire to be engaged with people, but he doesn't quite know how to get there, and his parents don't know how to get him out of the basement. Todd feels he's so far gone that he's angry at any push to get him with people. And Todd's parents have become so frustrated that they'd rather just leave him alone than rattle his cage.

The problem is that Todd hasn't been given any control over his life. And now, Mom and Dad aren't quite sure how to make the transfer. Todd needs to be pushed beyond his walls of isolation, and he'll need help pulling his head out of the sand. He needs to be gently and lovingly ushered out the door—even when he experiences pain, hurt, or rejection.

I talked with Todd about some new boundaries the family had adopted. The boundaries limited time in the basement and restricted Internet use to certain hours. New rules encouraged Todd to get a job, to participate in an extracurricular school activity, and to eat meals with the family. Dad prompted Todd to decide what he was going to do, to take the ball and run with it, knowing that Dad would help in any way Todd requested. They planned to meet once a week for breakfast to talk about how Todd was doing. Todd was given a timeline, a direction, and boundaries to keep within. Mom and Dad empowered him by giving him control.

Todd didn't like the changes at first. Change was hard—harder than everyone thought it would be. And they had a tough road for awhile. Putting rules into effect is one thing. Enforcing them is another. They had words as things became a little intense at times. But as Todd began taking control of his life, a new life unfurled for him that he had really always wanted, and he eventually began to enjoy it.

Retaking Control

At times a parent must retake control because a child just can't seem to make good decisions, and some of the choices have far-reaching consequences. You must take control when something else has taken control of your child. The way to determine whether you need to retake control is to ask a simple question: If your daughter continues on her present path, where will she be in six months? The answer to that question will determine whether you need to intervene.

Here are some situations that call for a parent's renewed involvement because the consequences could be ill-fated. The list is not exhaustive. These just happen to be things I have seen young people wrestle with and that demand attention.

First, if you begin to notice that your child seems depressed, is difficult to motivate, is unwilling to participate in life, and has suicidal thoughts and gestures, get him or her to a therapist or a hospital. Even if your child verbally downplays suicide, a teen's action might be speaking louder than words.

Second, drinking at a party is one thing. Showing up at school or work drunk or getting a DUI is another. Drinking at a party, which happens with about 90 percent of teens, can be corrected with the belief system and the related rules for inappropriate behavior. If your child continues to fail after repeated attempts to curb this behavior, pull in the boundaries a little, increase the consequences, or intervene with outside help.

Showing up at school or work drunk not only indicates a complete disregard for boundaries at home, it also shows a disregard for the rules of society. As a parent, teacher, youth worker, or just someone concerned for the welfare of this child, you must take stronger actions—now.

The same would hold true for drug use. Outside of a child smoking pot, you must take action immediately because of the plethora of drugs that are available and the intensity of the immediate addiction to those drugs.

Third, if you find that your child is being sexually abused by anyone, you must call the police or the appropriate state agency immediately, and the abuser should be removed from the environment quickly. The situation might even require a restraining order.

If you believe your child is being exploited by anyone or being deceived, whether in person or online, your intervention is necessary. You need to take control.

Fourth, when your children cannot control any of their habits, patterns, or actions, your intrusion or intercession is necessary, even if they don't want it.

We are seeing more and more teens involved with someone much older. When a 24-year-old hasn't matured and desires to hang around a 16-year-old, something is usually wrong. Formulate rules about the social relationships that are appropriate for your child. When those aren't in place and someone older becomes possessive or abusive with your child, your involvement is necessary. Running interference is justified.

Your teen's behavior may be a cry for your attention. If your child has one of these problems and you're hoping it will just go away, you're being irresponsible. These are times that you must act—quickly.

Giving Up Control

I've always thought that if parents spent less time trying to control their teens and more time helping them develop responsibility and maturity, their teens would be less rebellious and more mature. I've watched dads spend years trying to retain control of their kids and end up losing it anyway. And in the process, they lose their relationship with their kids. I've seen moms so fearful that their kids might do something wrong that they develop an unhealthy attachment. And they are unwilling to detach.

In order for children to become healthy adults, they will have to detach from Mom and Dad. Parents can build an environment that will empower their children to blossom in their next stage of life.

CHAPTER THIRTEEN

BUILDING MATURITY BY GIVING RESPONSIBILITY

Wouldn't you love to see your teen display mature and responsible behavior? Make good decisions? Use good judgment? Stand on good principles? Exhibit integrity? I've wrestled for years to come up with a formula for motivating immature kids to start thinking with maturity, sensibility, and wisdom.

I have concluded that maturity follows responsibility. This clarifies parents' immediate goal: to encourage their children to accept responsibility. How do they do that? By releasing control of their children's possible failure and by helping their children understand that the acceptance of responsibility develops the maturity they long for.

I'm amazed that so many parents want their teens to be mature yet retain a level of control that prevents their kids from taking on responsibility. Most parents probably don't retain that control intentionally. They retain that control because they desire to be involved in their kids' lives, but they do so by expressing that involvement through commands and a zealous desire to ensure their children don't make mistakes.

David Damico implies in his book *The Faces of Rage* that mistakes in raising kids aren't usually the reflection of parental error, as much as parental ignorance.[1] So true. Most mistakes aren't intentional; they are the result of just not knowing better, of trying to solve one problem and creating another.

In order for teens to be responsible, they have to be given something to be responsible for. They have to be given control. They have to be allowed to make decisions and choices. They must be able to exercise and practice their judgment. They do these things within the boundaries you set for their journey through their teen years. And they must be allowed to fail.

Oscar Wilde insightfully tells us, "Experience is the name everyone gives to their mistakes."[2] And if you want your relationship with your children to go deeper than it's ever been, stick with them when they fail or struggle to fulfill their obligations (a good sign of responsibility). Let your words become flesh, and be there to demonstrate your love for them—not to control but to guide.

James Belasco and Ralph Stayer state in their book *Flight of the Buffalo,* "Most of us overestimate the value of what we currently have, and have to give up, and underestimate the value of what we might gain."[3] I don't think I've ever heard someone say it any better.

Andy Law of the Creative Company stated that "Unless you are prepared to give up something valuable you will never be able to truly change at all, because you'll be forever in the control of things you can't give up."[4]

Helping your child become responsible requires that you give up control of your child—a control you don't really have anyway. You give them control and responsibility not because they've earned it but because they need it. Not because they demand it but because you want to give it. Not because they can handle all of it but because they need to learn to handle it all. If you try to keep control, your kids will always be irresponsible and will live out the consequences of not becoming mature.

If you are to help your children grow up, you must grow up as well. You help them grow, you let them grow, and you grow up with them. To show them how to get a life, you have to have a life. To encourage them to make wise choices, you have to make wise choices. To require that they act responsibly, you have to be responsible. The demand for them to mature calls for you to be mature. To demonstrate the need for change, you must be willing to share with them the changes in your life. That's a life-on-life experience that sharpens one another. Not just one but both.

When you create an atmosphere of change in relationship with your children, you plant within their hearts a hope that lets them see a future full of possibilities. Give it to them!

Rebecca

Rebecca's mom was determined to make up for all the ways she had failed her daughter. After all, she had given birth to Rebecca when she was only 15, allowed Rebecca's father to die, and never became the mother she always wanted to be, believing she had constantly failed her daughter. So Rebecca's mom determined to make up for all her mistakes by taking control of her daughter's life and making everything right.

Sounds futile, doesn't it? Sounds like this mother was preventing maturity by removing any opportunity for her child to accept responsibility. Rebecca was being controlled for well-intentioned but wrong reasons, and she was beginning to pay the price for her mother's conciliatory actions. Her mother was living through her daughter the life she had really wanted for herself as a teen. She assumed that if she only had a mother who was like her while she was a teen, she would not have gone through what she did. She was determined to make sure her daughter wasn't going to have to live as she had. So she controlled everything, and Rebecca wasn't responsible for anything.

Rebecca was growing more and more immature as the days passed. A daughter who was once motivated to take responsibility for her life as a 14-year-old had been reduced to a frustrated young (very young) 18-year-old who would rather stay at Heartlight than go home. She had even been pushed to cutting on herself to express her frustration over her mother's overly controlling sovereignty cloaked in acts of service.

Mom didn't have a clue…still doesn't. She just doesn't understand how a daughter who has had a mother like her would ever end up in the place she's in. She would always tearfully comment, "I did everything for her." That she did. And Rebecca's attempts to share her frustration with her mother fell on deaf ears. The relationship began to show the strain of her mom's total control, and Rebecca moved on to where she could take control of her life, grab responsibility by the horns, and live the life that God intended. Cutting the umbilical cord to Mom was a hard but necessary move.

It was harder on Mom. She still calls regularly asking what she can do to get her daughter back. There's nothing she can do. The problem is what she didn't do by not giving her daughter responsibility for her own life. Her mom's control has had some pretty far-reaching effects and has moved Mom to a place that she didn't want to be. In time, with Rebecca's maturity and longing to have a family, perhaps the relationship will be healed and restored. I am hopeful that, in time, Rebecca will get to enjoy that.

The sad part is that Rebecca's mom lost her daughter by trying to give her daughter something she had never had, to prove her worthiness as a mother through her daughter.

Some of the most mature and wise adults I know are those who went through horrendous times during their adolescent years. Crime, divorce, death of parents, and abandonment created environments where the victims had to accept responsibility for their lives in order to survive. Kids never cease to amaze me in their resiliency and ability to adapt to horrific situations or circumstances that required them to take on responsibility prematurely. Just about every kid I know who has experienced this level of adversity has stepped up to the plate, swung well, and hit a few homers. It doesn't mean they haven't also grounded out, hit a pop fly, or get thrown out at the plate. But they chose to be in the game and play their positions. When forced to assume responsibility for their lives, these young people have done well. Your child is capable of the same.

I encourage parents to give their children things that are treasured and valued now instead of waiting to leave those valued things in an inheritance when they die. You're going to give it to them anyway, so why not give it while the act of giving can strengthen the relationship and demonstrate how much you value your child—even when they don't deserve it? Must a child always do well to receive their parents' grace? Grace wouldn't be called grace if that were true, would it?

Giving It to Them

Believe it or not, most teens develop maturity from the outside in. We clothe them in maturity, trusting that it will be internalized. For teens, the one thing worse than not getting what you want is this: getting what you want too easily. Teens do want control; they just fear the responsibility that comes along with it. That responsibility must be handed to them so they can have control.

I talked with a lady in the Toledo, Ohio, airport who asked me if I knew what the greatest gift parents could give their children might be. As I thought, she injected, "Make them get a job. It will teach them lessons about responsibility in life they should have learned at home."

Sadly, she may be correct because nowadays the home is rarely the place where responsibility is developed. Perhaps issues of control are not defined in the home as they should be. In the workplace, workers know their jobs and have managers who have authority. Correction is not an issue. Employees know who writes the paycheck. Do your kids know what they're working for? Do they know why you are transferring things to them and requiring things of them?

You must empower them to make decisions, telling them they have the freedom to choose from the options you line out. Communicate that intention with phrases like "You choose," "That's your choice," "It's up to you," "I'll support you in whatever you decide," "Hey, you're the man—you make the call," or "Sweetheart, this is something you're going to have to decide." Give them the chance to exercise their judgment.

When you empower your children this way you affirm them—and open the door to the possibility that they just might make the wrong decision. Sometimes you need to let them fail, even knowing that you could have made things right by intervening. For instance, you could have forced your 14-year-old son to finish mowing the yard before dark by reminding him repeatedly. But perhaps the greater lesson will be that by not getting it finished before dark, he would have a consequence for not doing what he said he would do. What do you think is the greater value?

Or when your 18-year-old daughter hasn't applied for college, you could force her to apply by getting on her constantly to fill out all the applications. You could make her do it now. But maybe the best thing is just to tell her once, place the needed papers in her room, and then leave it alone. If she fills them out and gets accepted, then you've not wasted some good breath nagging her, and she learned to get it done on her own timetable. On the other hand, she may not get accepted because she didn't turn in her application. But the greater lesson she may need to learn is that she must take responsibility for what she wants to do in life. She also learns to complete a task, to respect the school's requirements, and to expect consequences. The lessons really are unlimited and come best when your child is given responsibility and has no recourse or escape from the resulting consequences.

Give your children the freedom to make their decisions about academics. I tell young people all the time that whether or not they graduate from high school is up to them. You might help them any way you can. Or you may support them any way they ask. But you cannot be responsible for their academics—it's their responsibility.

When your child goes off to school, you may still have boundaries in place for their college years. If you think that your child is extremely immature, send him to a small Christian school with more boundaries than a larger state school. Tell him that you'll pay for him to go to school at one of four particular colleges (that's your boundary), and he gets to choose which one he goes to (that's his responsibility).

When your child has decided to get a job during school, let him decide his work hours so he will have to juggle his school activities and social life. He'll learn to balance his time schedule and budget his money. Let him handle the issues at work: how to balance demands at home with demands at work, how to negotiate with a boss, and how to be a part of a family. Aren't these the same issues that married couples deal with? Aren't these the type of issues that couples with kids struggle with to find a balance? Maintaining relationships is vital during the difficult teen years, but so is training your child to be successful.

You are not disengaging when you tell them that they must be responsible for some of their own decisions. And furthermore, as long as the "money highway" is operating between you and your children, you have the right to give them money with some strings attached. But they must choose whether they continue to get money from you. And they should submit to the conditions of the agreement to get funds, or you will void the "contract."

I encourage families to give their children a checkbook in the eighth grade. After figuring out how much you're going to spend on each child in a month for school supplies, lunches, allowance, clothes, and special-event money, give it to them in an account. Your children might just surprise you. Your daughter will either do very well and balance her funds or come home from the mall with a $200 pair of jeans that have some special design on them, which she will now have to wear every day for the next year because she has no more money for clothes. Matter of fact, she might not have enough money to buy lunch or go on that special event she wanted to go on.

But this is where the learning takes place—unless you bail her out by giving her more money. If you do, she will never realize where she has failed and will only have to learn another way. If she needs lunch money, I would suggest that she wear some old jeans to school and rent out her new $200 pair (kids' ingenuity never ceases to amaze me). When you do this, you're giving your child responsibility. You're giving her the ability to make choices. And you're helping her learn about decision making. And if she fails, let her feel the consequences. I've yet to hear of a teen starving to death while wearing a $200 pair of jeans. It's a training opportunity that might save her life, her marriage, or her relationship with her own kids one day. This is how a teen gathers wisdom.

Give kids the responsibility to do their own laundry. Give them more than you think they can handle. Let them make decisions. Let them feel what it's like now to live in a world where they need to set boundaries. Kids are resilient. They want to make decisions. They want to be in control. Give it to them.

Jim

Sometimes, giving an answer to a question prevents the one who poses the question from having to do the work to find the answer. The search may be more significant than the find, so giving answers may undercut responsibility. This was certainly the case for Jim, whose mother wouldn't quit answering questions...whether they were questions posed to her or to other people. She was amazing. If she heard a question, she answered it regardless of whom it was directed to.

As a result, Jim never had to look for the answers to anything. So as a 17-year-old, he didn't know how to figure anything out—answers, solutions, remedies to situations, wisdom, or keys to the future. His mother's incessant answers to every question and her justification of Jim's inappropriate behavior were amazing. Jim is a nice young man, but he is frightened by the thought of not being able to live on his own. He should be.

I encouraged his mother over a period of months to let Jim seek his own answers. Unfortunately, Jim had shut down and wasn't motivated even to ask questions. Yes, she had even begun to tell him the questions he needed to be asking and was giving the answers—all in the same breath.

When teens ask questions, parents can easily give answers and steer the conversation in the "right" direction. But easy answers and declarations stifle relationships. When kids want to talk, the last thing they need is to be preached at.

Answering all your child's questions can also preclude wonderment and creativity, take away the responsibility to find an answer, and stop the search with you. Think about the value of putting a puzzle together, hunting for Easter eggs, seeking out information for a research project, or doing a crossword puzzle. The fun and excitement of each of these is in the search, not in the end result. I've taken Mensa intelligence tests in airline magazines just to make sure I still have the ability to think (it's questionable at times). If I cheat by jumping to the answers listed on the next page, the search is immediately over. Providing answers to your teens' questions will at times stop some very good and needed processes. The journey is usually more valuable than the goal.

To find out how much you are in the habit of answering your teen's questions, spend the weekend not saying a word unless you are spoken to and strive to only answer questions with questions. Don't give your opinion for a weekend. This little exercise will show you how much your teen hangs on to your answers and thinking. If you want your child to be an independent thinker and to use his head as you give him more responsibility, you must wean him from an unhealthy dependency on you.

One way to help train kids to assume responsibility is to stop reminding them of appointments posted on the refrigerator calendar. They're capable of looking at a calendar. And quit waking them up to go to school. They're old enough to set an alarm and get out of bed by themselves. Most young people want to graduate from high school and will do what's necessary to make that happen. Your child may oversleep on occasion as he gets used to getting up on his own, but he will learn.

You are not responsible for his job. He is. And you are not responsible to do his laundry. He is.

I hope that you understand that I'm *not* saying to stop spending time with your kids, to ignore their needs, or to fail to engage with them when you are invited into their space. Remain engaged in every way. Rather, gradually give up the responsibility you carry for your kids. If you will transfer that responsibility to them, you will lead them to maturity.

What If They Won't Take It?

Transferring responsibility to your child is especially important if you are dealing with a child who is struggling. This is usually a very awkward and confusing situation because parents are reluctant to let kids assume responsibility for their lives when the kids are acting so irresponsibly. And it is further complicated when parents have to take control because the kids are spinning out of control. Parents have to do what they have to do when their kids' behavior has some possible far-reaching and life-threatening consequences. But parents' short-term control should lead to the long-term goal of helping kids accept responsibility for their own lives.

Continue to focus on your belief system, your authority in the house as a parent, and your desire to see your child grow and understand the importance of consequences. Let me give you an example. Let's say that your child comes home drunk—again. You might find a time to say something like this:

> Sarah, we need to discuss some things that you and I know aren't in line with what we've all agreed to about the use of alcohol. This has happened a number of times before, so you're forcing me to take your car away, not because I don't want you to drive but because that's what we agreed to. What I've been doing doesn't seem to be working, but I can't just sit back and do nothing as I watch my daughter go on a path that will destroy her. I'm not going to let that happen. That wouldn't be loving you. We're going to get a counselor involved, and until he or she gives me a "thumbs up" that you can commit to quit drinking, you're going to be grounded, and I need your keys to the car. I applaud you for getting someone else to drive, but your continual reckless behavior is causing me to have to act. You'll get the car back when I know that you've gone six weekends without drinking when you're not grounded. You have to understand that I'm not going to just sit back and watch you continually exercise bad judgment. If you continue to do what you're doing, you're going to end up in a place that you don't want to be, so I'm going to work my hardest to make sure that doesn't happen. I'm fighting for you, and I won't stop because I love you too much to let you destroy your life.

A statement like this is an affirmation of your relationship with your daughter, and it has some bite to it. It tells Sarah that "This isn't about me, it's about you, sweetheart."

Be ready for her to shift the blame. "But Dad, all I had was one drink. Someone must have put more alcohol in the punch." "Dad, that cop would've never known I was drunk if you had fixed the taillight on the car." "It's not my fault they have these stupid laws." "Well, if Sharon would have brought me home when she said she would, I wouldn't have been drunk, and you would have never known." Here's your response: "This is your deal, sweetheart. You are responsible for yourself. I really don't care about what anyone else did or didn't do. This is about you, your life, and what is required of you."

Or she may try to justify it all. "Dad, everyone in my class drinks. You and Mom make these rules that are so stupid." "Sally's parents let her drink, and she's 16, so I thought it would be okay." "It was Sean's birthday, and we just celebrated." "It was just this one time, Dad." "I waited to drive home, Dad." "I'm almost 18, Dad. Didn't you drink when you were 18?" "I'm going to drink, and you're not going to stop me."

Or she may try to give excuses. "I couldn't quit." "I felt pressured." "I didn't know alcohol was there." "I thought it was Pepsi and didn't know there was vodka in the drink." "Sean gave it to me and didn't tell me." "There's nothing wrong with what I did, so if you and Mom want to just carry out your little rules, then fine." "Whatever!"

Or she may try to minimize what has just happened. "Come on, Dad, it's not that big of a deal." "You and Mom are trying to make this bigger than it is." "I don't need a counselor! It's not like I have a drinking problem or something." "Just four beers, Dad; it's not like I was really drunk or something."

Whatever she says, your message remains the same. Keep focused on the bigger picture when caught in this barrage of blame shifting, justification, excuses, or minimizing of the behavior. And remember, the bigger picture is not about drinking, it's about responsibility. This would be my response to Sarah:

> It's not about being drunk; it's about respect for what we've all agreed to. It's not about someone else, it's

about you. This is your deal. It's no one else's fault. It is a problem because it continues to happen. And no excuse will ever move me to say that what you did was okay. You and I both agreed that we didn't want to be on this path, and I'm not giving up my part of the agreement just because you want to back out. You chose to lose the car because that's what we agreed to. You chose to be grounded because that's what we agreed to. You chose your own consequences. And you want me to let those go? You're making some pretty irresponsible choices. You can't pin this on anyone other than yourself, Sarah. I'm sorry you've put yourself in this position.

Can you hear the real message behind these words? "I want you to be responsible. And because you're involved in something that could eventually control you, we're going to bump up the consequences a little."

Remember that the presenting behavior is usually not the underlying problem, so the next conversation may be spent dealing with that. But two separate things are happening, and you need to be careful not to confuse those things. When a child comes home drunk, that may not be the time to talk about the underlying issues. And when the time is right to talk about the underlying issues, don't ask, "How many drinks did you have at that party on May third at 1:00 AM when you were with Sean and Sally?" Keep the issues separate and deal with each of them differently. Stay strong on the behavior and the assumption of responsibility and softer on the motivating factors for the behavior.

Maturity

Maturity is a character trait that combines being experienced, wise, well-versed, grounded, and knowledgeable. Maturity happens as a result of being responsible. And it is something we all want to see in our kids. It assures parents that they have done well in their child rearing. It is a character trait that will be carried throughout the rest of a child's life. But it only happens when parents create an environment that encourages and sometimes demands responsibility from their children.

CHAPTER FOURTEEN

WE'RE SPINNING OUT OF CONTROL

One of parents' worst nightmares is to see their families spinning out of control, to be unable to stop the rapid descent into a full-fledged crash.

If you are currently experiencing that feeling of helplessness, hopelessness, and fear, I strongly encourage you to take action. Talk to someone—a friend, pastor, youth minister, counselor, parent, or mentor. You need to gain wisdom regarding your situation, so ask for help. And stop at nothing until you find an answer. The course you take when your child is in this wild and unrestrained situation just might determine whether your future will include him or her.

Choosing to Intervene

Three stages take you to a point of intervention, where you involve someone else in your family's business. The first stage is accepting what is actually happening within your family. The second stage is justifying the intervention. And the third stage is plotting a course and pulling your child out of his or her nosedive.

Accepting the reality of the problem is difficult for some parents. Many just can't acknowledge or recognize the severity of the problem. Parents who see only the good, hope for the best, and believe no wrong are usually blind to what everyone around them can already see. Admittedly, because problems often develop gradually, the family can easily not realize how serious they are. Friends, neighbors, and those around the family can see what's happening, but they may not know how to convince the parents of something they don't see. If you find yourself in this situation, don't hesitate to go to those around you for counsel. They know what's going on.

That forms the foundation to the second stage, justifying the intervention. Other people will agree with your decision to intervene in some way, encouraging you to do something. You will need this support as you take the next step.

The third stage is a little lonelier, especially if you have to remove your child from the home. Most parents I meet mention that when the decision came down to removing their child from the home, they felt quite isolated and sometimes even excommunicated. Taking action can be painful, and most people avoid pain. Friends will describe your situation to others as a sad time, a painful time, and as a time they hope they don't have to go through with their children. Their description will be accurate.

Teens are out of control when they don't have the internal ability to function externally within the established boundaries and rules of a home. The resulting behaviors, if allowed to continue, could have some dangerous or grave consequences.

Regardless of the reason behind the behavior, intervention is necessary to protect the child and deal with the issues that led to the behavior. I'm sure you've had plenty of conversations with your child about your concerns. Perhaps you've even implemented boundaries and helped your child understand consequences. If you haven't, I suggest that you do so quickly.

But at some point, when all else has failed, you are the one who will need to make some decisions about the next step. What your child thinks is somewhat immaterial as he or she is obviously not thinking well.

This is not the time to spend mulling over where everything has gone wrong. It's not a time to shift the blame, make accusations, question motives, or withdraw and disengage from your child. It's a time for action. It's not a time for determining whether you are a failure as a parent, but it's a time to make sure you don't fail to help your child at a time when he or she needs you most.

Do We Need Help?

Often parents will struggle to determine if their children need help. Has your child's behavior deteriorated in the last six months? Do you have reason to believe it won't continue to worsen in the next six months?

Your first line of offense with your out-of-control teen is to utilize the resources around you. Perhaps this first line will ward off any further difficulty and pull your child out of the nosedive. That first line might include your child's teachers, the school administration, a Sunday school teacher, other parents of kids at church, your pastor, your parents, your siblings, your friends, your Bible study group, a counseling hot line, the older couple down the street, a youth minister, a Young Life leader…just about anyone who has had contact with your child. Even his or her friends. In fact, if your teen's friends show up at your home, don't be afraid to ask them what's going on. Some won't be afraid to answer; they might be concerned as well. Just make sure you ask questions, and ask people to be honest with you.

Voltaire once said, "Common sense is not so common." An old Chinese proverb says, "He who asks is a fool for five minutes, but he who does not ask remains a fool forever." And you'll read in Proverbs 15:22 (NIV), "Plans fail for lack of counsel, but with many advisers they succeed." After you've had time to get counsel and you've had some time to think it through, start to put your plan into action.

Perhaps your child needs to go to counseling. If so, then put that requirement into your rules or belief system at home. And if the counselor determines that your child needs some type of medication, then trust what the counselor is saying and go see a psychiatrist who understands teens and their issues. Try to surround yourself with people you trust, so that when you ask for their counsel and they tell you what you don't want to hear, you can trust them anyway. If you pick and choose the counsel you receive, you'll more than likely just continue to do what you want, and your child will continue to spin out of control. Don't let old beliefs about medicine control your new decisions. If your child is depressed, A.D.D., hyperactive, unable to sleep at night, bipolar, overly anxious, or has a mental condition that demands medication, don't let your outdated boundaries keep you from getting your child help.

Hospitalization is needed whenever children might harm themselves. Extreme cutting, bizarre behavior, extreme depression, suicidal thoughts, or excessive drug or alcohol use are just a few of the symptoms that might warrant hospitalization. Don't hesitate to hospitalize your child just because you don't know what the problem is. It's better to be safe than sorry.

Residential Programs

If all your efforts are fruitless and you begin to see that your child is not responding to any of these "at home" interventions, it's time to consider placing your teen in an alternative residential setting. No doubt this will be one of the hardest decisions you'll ever have to make. Having a child leave home is not an easy decision, nor is it a small task. But once you make the decision, you can begin the search for the right placement.

You have many options to consider. I am quite biased toward our residential program, Heartlight Ministries in Hallsville, Texas, but other programs offer different formats that might fit your needs better. A wilderness camp works well for rebellious kids who need something to get their attention. They are usually 30- to 60-day programs that remove kids from drug or alcohol environments and allow them to spend time talking, reflecting, and confronting in an environment that is controlled by natural boundaries. Those who participate in wilderness programs usually need some type of follow-up residential program. The two programs complement each other and, in the long run, end up saving time and money.

As I mentioned above, hospitalization is needed when kids endanger themselves or are having severe alcohol or drug problems and need to detoxify and get medical intervention. This stay is usually a temporary "hold" until you can find a long-term program.

Therapeutic boarding schools include counseling or small-group therapy. They also address therapeutic and educational needs of each resident. Heartlight would also be classified as a therapeutic boarding school.

Some programs operate overseas. Explore any program like this carefully, paying special attention to the staff of the program. Make sure you meet those who will be supervising your child. Moving a problem child to another country with minimum compliance standards is not always the answer to your teen's needs. This may prevent your involvement with your child and not give your child the adequate experience he or she needs.

To find out more information about alternatives, explore the Internet and review the materials for each program. Ask the difficult questions and make sure you visit the campus before placing your child anywhere.

How Did They Know?

Parents realize the need to take action in different ways. The progression is usually the same: They come to the stark reality that their situations with their teens are out of control, their attempts to help aren't working, and their predicaments demand immediate attention.

A while back I asked families that were currently with us at Heartlight to complete this sentence: I knew my child was spinning out of control when——. Here are some of their responses:

- "...everything got crazy. The cell phone bill listed daily phone calls from 1:00 to 3:00 AM, and her only response was, 'So what?' She started running away and said that her two-year-old sister unlocked all the downstairs windows so she could sneak back in late at night. The brand-new shoes I bought for an anniversary cruise were suddenly missing after she told me how 'hot' they were and that all her friends wanted them. I can go on and on...the list never quits. We were helpless."

- "...our entire family was being controlled by her behavior. My marriage was failing, my relationship with my older daughter was suffering, I wasn't eating, sleeping, or performing well at work. I was beginning to withdraw from social settings as well and felt like my family was falling apart. Every option I tried had failed."

- "...she stopped smiling and refused to get up and go to school."

- "...her attitude changed. She was more argumentative and more defiant. She began hanging out with a different group of kids, who I later found out were experimenting with drugs and alcohol."

- "...he became as physical as he was verbal!"

- "...he began hanging out with a pretty rough crew. That's when his attitude towards us as parents made a complete change overnight, and he began to hate everything we said or did."

- "...she began cutting and was obsessed with killing herself in order to go to heaven to be with her dad. I was afraid to leave her alone. She was a sad little girl. She was meeting with a therapist, her youth minister, her Sunday school teacher, and her school counselor, and they were all taking extra time with her and pouring their lives into her. All of these 'interventions' weren't effective. One night she came right out and said, 'I need more help. I have no more desire to live or stop cutting than I did before everyone started helping me. I just want to die; I don't like feeling this way.'"

- "... I realized I had exhausted all of the parental tools I had to control the direction of her life."

- "...she couldn't get over her dad's death. Her depression was in control. She wanted help more than I wanted it for her and begged me to find her a place where she could get it."

- "...she looked me in the eye and said, 'I'm going to do whatever I want and there isn't a thing you can do about it!'"

- "…he was arrested three times in three months for possession of marijuana, and he chose to go to juvenile detention center rather than come home and be under house arrest. He had violated the plan we had set in place, and he knew that if he defied me again, he was going to have to leave. The situation was tough, but the decision was easy. He made it for me."

- "…our son was not responding to our efforts to help him. He ran away from home for the second time and was brought home by the local police. Our efforts at changing schools and participating in family counseling with him for the previous four months weren't helping, and our counselor recommended we find a different place for him to live."

- "…she started cutting herself and continued to cut school even in the face of probation."

- "…I looked into his big brown eyes and the spark that had always been there was gone. All I saw was a look of hopelessness and darkness, a silent crying out for help. I knew it was time to search for something or someone to help bring that spark of light and hope back into my son's eyes."

- "…he became disrespectful to his parents, his sisters, his teachers, his stepparents. He was abusive, verbally and possibly physically, to his girlfriends. He left school when he wanted and was suspended."

- "…my son looked at my wife and said, 'If you don't shut your mouth, I'll shut if for you.'"

- "…we were calling the police several times a week, not knowing if or when she was coming home. We never knew whom she was with or where she was. The police told us to do something now or things will only get worse."

- "…my daughter came into my bedroom late one night. She was crying and said, 'Mom and Dad, I need help.'"

- "…our son was ignoring everything we said, did everything we didn't want him to do, and said nasty things we never thought would come out of his mouth."

When It's Time

The following checklist includes some behaviors that reveal the possible need to place your child outside your home.

- When your teen won't listen to reason, and he is becoming increasingly disrespectful, dishonest, and disobedient, openly displaying his rebellious actions.

- When there is physical contact or threats.

- When a habit has engulfed your child.

- When your child is displaying behavior that is a marked change from what was normal (sleeping longer, forgetfulness, lack of motivation, depression, hating what they once loved, and loving what they once hated).

- When your child blatantly ignores or profoundly rebels against your boundaries, belief system, or rules of the home. This can be shown in passive-aggressive or openly defiant behavior.

- When your teen is too depressed to function within normal requests at home.

- When your child has no conscience about his actions, the consequences, or the effect on himself or other family members.

- When suicidal thoughts and comments arise.

- When your child treats people, pets, or belongings, in a threatening or overly unruly way.

- When your child's behavior puts him or her in danger or at high risk.

- When posttraumatic behaviors of drinking, taking drugs, or being sexually active are present.

- When your teen's continued disregard for others in the family is causing strife, sleepless nights, and trauma to other siblings, and you can't stop it.

This checklist is not exhaustive, but these seem to be the common reasons parents place children outside their home.

Chris

When people are in pain, they do pretty weird things. The first time I picked up a child to come live in our residential program, I flew to Nashville, Tennessee. I met Chris' father at the airport, and he told me his son was at a local park, and that was where we were going to pick him up. Chris' dad and I expected that Chris, when confronted, would probably cry a little, yell and scream a little, and then reluctantly come with me.

It was a great idea, but it didn't quite work that way. The minute Chris and I were introduced and his dad said, "Mark is going to take you back to Texas with him," I caught a right jab to my right eye and cheekbone that knocked me to the ground. It was the only time I have ever seen stars during the light of day! I ended up with a big black eye. As I was coming to, I rolled over to watch Chris running through the woods to get away from me, and I heard his dad say, "I guess we should have done something different." *Imagine that,* I thought to myself.

As we walked back to the car to discuss plan B, I caught myself asking God, *You've called me to this?* But I learned a great lesson. And I've never been hit again.

The lesson was this: Be prepared. People in pain do some pretty weird things. To make a long story short, I got back on the plane that night alone. Two days later, my eye was still black, and my cheek was still swollen, but Chris moved into the guys' house. He apologized, and we got along fine for years. Whenever I think of Chris I wink my eye. He doesn't remember what happened. He was higher than a kite that day. And whenever I hear someone say, "We should do something different," I think of Chris' dad. Be prepared for anything as you encounter a teen out of control.

Phil

I learned a second lesson about confronting kids for the first time. Phil's parents had asked that I pick him up at their home, and they assured me he would be there. They didn't tell me he had run away a few days earlier. They feared I wouldn't come if I knew they really didn't know where he was.

When I arrived at their home, they told me that he was at a KISS concert and that he would be easy to find because they knew where he was sitting and because he had red hair. Sounded good to me. I sat in the parking lot, strategizing the best way to get him to come out with me. In my immature brilliance, I decided to tell him that his parents were in an accident, and I was sent to pick him up and take him home. As I walked into the concert, I couldn't hear myself think because the music was so loud. It was dark, and all I had was a picture of the young man. After an hour of squinting, I finally found him. I walked up to him and noticed he was drunk. I thought to myself that his condition would work in my favor because he wouldn't be thinking too well. It worked. He walked out with me. And as we started to drive, I shared with him that we would drive for five hours to a program where we could help him.

Here's the lesson. Because I lied to him, he never trusted me. Phil never connected with me or anyone. And I put it all back on the way I brought him there. The lesson? Don't lie when you're in a difficult situation with your child. It will come back and bite you at a later date.

Will

And I learned a third lesson. I drove to Little Rock, Arkansas, with a fellow who knew of a family that had a son who was messed up in drugs again. We were going to pick him up and take him back home with us. When we confronted Will, he ran from us, cussing at the top of his lungs. He slipped on a dishrag on the floor and hit his head against the cabinets. While we were sitting at the hospital waiting for him to get stitched up, I asked again, *Lord, you've called me to this?* (I asked myself that a lot in the early days of working with kids.)

Will got in the backseat of the car, and we drove a few hours home. I thought I'd botched everything. But in the back of my 1982 white Ford Bronco, Will accepted Christ. On his own. And he calls the scar on his cheek his "Jesus Scar." Third lesson: Stand firm. Even though someone runs, something goes bad, or someone cusses at you, God can bring that person to a relationship with Him. I think of Will whenever I see a white Bronco.

Be Prepared. Don't Lie. Stand Firm. Some good wisdom for those preparing to battle for the lives of their children. Love is sometimes tough. And your efforts to save the life of your child will never be forgotten.

CHAPTER FIFTEEN

Hope in a Difficult Time

We grew up in a generation that was bent on peace, didn't we? The peace emblem was on every black light poster and tie-dyed shirt I had. It was our age of "give peace a chance," peace movements, and peace rallies. Peace was promoted in relationships, flashed with our *V* signs, and yelled from the rooftops in our pursuit of world harmony.

I watched a television commercial the other day that stated, "We put the meaning in meaningful relationships." And we did. And while we "peaced" everything together, we threw out something pretty important—the concept of allowing relationships to survive conflict. We were so bent to find oneness that we ran from anything of conflict, struggle, and hardship. And in doing so, our generation ran from marriages, denied anything negative was happening to our children, and created a generation gap of a different sort than what we experienced as adolescents.

That absence of struggle has kept relationships from moving to the depth we really longed for. The relationship pendulum has moved far to one side, pointing to peace at all costs. Our longing for peace made our generation run from conflict. Divorce rates have never been as high as they have been the last 25 years. Sadly, many of the family struggles of today are the result of my generation's well-intentioned pursuit to "put the meaning into meaningful relationships," which has unintentionally caused much heartache and hurt as people have disappeared during difficult times. No wonder children feel that they'll be abandoned when they're in conflict—that's what they have seen growing up. Why would they think any differently?

Is there hope? Yes, there is. Hope for a peace that allows the conflict and struggle in our lives to lead us to stronger and deeper relationships with those we love. The world's view of peace is the absence of conflict. God's definition of peace is hope in the midst of the conflict. On the other side of this current crisis or impending hardship with your teen, you'll be fine, and you may even be better.

I recently walked up to a family who had lost their son the night before. I told them how sorry I was that they had to go through something like this. I shared my shock, my grief, and my hurt, all the time assuring them that God would get them through this difficult time. The boy's dad looked at me and said, "I don't think I can do this" with tears streaming down his face. I could barely get the words out from the flood of emotion I was feeling as I cried with him. "Ben," I said, "if I had told you yesterday that your son was going to die tonight—" He interrupted me with the words, "I think I would have told you I couldn't handle that." He paused for me to enter back into the conversation. "That's the point. You didn't think you could, but you did. And you'll make it to the other side of this tragedy, and God will walk you through it and be with you the whole way. I promise."

I've led Young Life groups in which kids have died, and I've sat with the lost families who've experienced such excruciating pain. It tore me up, and even now, I tear up just thinking about the losses those families have experienced. I've buried kids whom I have loved, kids with whom I had experienced many good times—all victims of malice, accidents, or cancer. I've sat for hours with parents who felt as if they couldn't go on, but they did.

My wife and I have had more than 1500 kids live with us through the years, all of whom have struggled immensely. I've shed many tears with their parents, who, at the time, didn't see the path to make it through the struggle, but they did.

I've had thousands of counseling sessions, phone conversations, and conference calls with moms and dads who were worn out. They were so tired of being called every name in the book, challenged on every thought they've ever had, and absolutely depleted because of all the hardship caused by their teen. All believed they weren't going to survive what was before them, but they did.

I've given just about every weekend of my life to families across this country, speaking at seminars for parents caught in family crises, parents feeling as if their world were falling apart. Many had lost hope and didn't think they were going to make it, but they did.

I talk to people on radio interviews, in airports, at churches, when I'm out to eat, and wherever I speak. So many are desperate, looking for answers to the questions their teens' behaviors pose. Many thought they would never get past this traumatic experience of their teen spinning out of control, but they did.

And just as they have, so will you.

My college degree is in finance, with an emphasis in investments. And I know this: There is no greater investment you can make than investing in the life of your child. And even though the market may be down and you're not seeing the return you had hoped for, now is not the time to bail out.

Your child's potential is still captured in that thumbprint of our heavenly Father, who knew where to place His treasure. And it was with you. And the time you give and the effort that you invest will one day pay off. And the payoff will be great.

You are investing in your teen, in your teen's future marriage, in your future daughter- or son-in-law, in your future grandchildren, in the life that God has given you. So don't bail. Keep your interest high and make your investment one of longevity. Paul reminds us of our return in Galatians 6:9 (NIV): "Let us not become weary in doing good, for at the proper time we will reap a harvest if we do not give up."

What Does Hope Look Like?

I heard a story years ago about Abraham Lincoln leaving a church service on a Sunday afternoon. It was raining horrendously and had evidently been raining for quite some time. As he and a colleague were leaving the church, surveying the downpour, his colleague asked, "Think it will *ever* quit?" President Lincoln's two-word answer helps me through tough times, whether mine or those around me. He profoundly answered, "Always does."

Somehow, just knowing that whatever pain I feel will pass helps me endure the pain I am experiencing. Tell me it will be over. Tell me that the dentist drilling on my tooth will finish soon. Assure me that the grief I feel will leave. Just promise me that this momentary and light affliction will be over one day. Swear to me that the hurt and pain I feel will quit.

"Always does."

When I meet with families who are in need of help with their teens, I lay an important foundational perspective: I'm more concerned with their teens five years from now than I am with getting them through the current difficulty. The inappropriate behavior of their children may have forced these parents to sit across from me to try and figure out a solution, but that is not the focus of our conversation. Sure, the inappropriate behavior must stop, but the real question for me is, "what must you do today to ensure that your child has a great relationship with you five years from now? And in most cases, families do manage to get through the difficult days, and the troubled teen and his or her parents end up having a great relationship in the future.

Why Try?

Parents often ask me, "So if my child is going to get through the issues anyway, and we're all going to be fine, then why even work at dealing with the issues?" That's a good question that deserves an answer. Here's an analogy:

A man is rushed to the hospital suffering a stroke. He gets to the emergency room, and the doctor looks at him and says, "I think there is hope for a good outcome with your condition—if you use the medication we have available." So the family is incredibly encouraged and full of hope. But no one does anything. They don't use the medication. People just sit around doing nothing. So the man's condition deteriorates, and the family begins to lose hope.

Hope depends on our actions. If you don't do anything, there is very little hope of changing the outcome.

Timing is key. You must act quickly. You must be willing to work on the issues in front of you if you are to create a hopeful situation. If you do nothing, you will incur the consequences and damage resulting from your lack of action. In other words, you can't just sit back and hope as you do nothing. You must get engaged and be a part of the process. If you do, you have the hope of restored relationships and mended connections.

The way you manage this process is more important than just getting through this time. How you relate to and interact with your children during this difficult time will determine the quality of your relationship with them in the future. How you stand with them during this difficult time will determine the amount of time your children spend in darkness and the amount of damage they suffer as they struggle through their issues.

What I want you to understand is this: There isn't much hope for those parents who willingly sit back and do nothing when their children are struggling and in the process of destroying their lives. But those parents who are actively involved with their children during the struggle usually move on to have great relationships with their kids.

What If...

The next question I often hear is, "What if my child never changes?" That's a harder question to answer. Sometimes a teen just doesn't change. The way they are now is the way they will be in 20 years. As much as I would like to tell you that everyone I've ever met with is doing well, I have to tell you that a few still struggle. Thankfully, the number of those that fit that category is small.

What's the hope in this situation? That you would be willing to change your perspective, your expectations, and perhaps your dreams for your child. There are some things you can never change. As painful as this may be to hear, believing has nothing to do with it. You can hope all you want and believe all you want, but it's not going to change anything.

Hope will come as you change your dreams, your hopes, and your expectations for your child. While that realization is tough to accept sometimes, many times parents feel a great relief as they finally embrace who their children really are. They release the frustration and aggravation they have felt watching their children openly defy their expectations. I pray that God will give you a new vision for your child and that you will learn to love him or her in ways that you never have, always giving them a taste of God's loving and gracious character and a touch of His love in a higher hope that one day God will welcome them into His arms and touch their hearts in a way that only He can.

What You Can Grab Onto

You will gain confidence as you engage the process and do what you know to do. Gain an understanding of why your child does what he does, develop a belief system, get your house in order, set the boundaries, be strong when you need to be strong, learn to be sensitive, allow pain to have its full effect, and deal with your own issues that might have played a part in your child's struggles. Pray, engage with your child, and hope that something will take root to move your teen to maturity and responsibility and that you will be able to restore your relationship with him or her.

Do what you need to do. Take control of those things over which you do have control. And then wait with anticipation.

Bentley

Bentley sat across from me at a local coffee shop and shared with me how he hated his parents, was being rebellious, had done some pretty stupid things, but now he wanted to get back into relationship with them. I asked, "Why?" His answer was simple. He said, "I don't want to be one of those 30-year-old guys who sits around and complains about his parents. I want to resolve things now." I was astounded at his willingness to make some changes. He was committed to change without me having to convince him that he needed to change. Bentley was seeking help, looking for counsel, and starting to turn back to his parents. I wish all of the young people I have counseled over the years would be so easy.

Hope came easily for Bentley's parents because they saw evidence of his desire to change. After a year, Bentley was back in control, and his parents saw what they would end up calling a yearlong turnaround. By God's grace, Bentley was able to straighten his life out.

Usually a turnaround takes longer. Most teens have to be taught that they need to change, and they have to be taught *how* to change. Once that is in place, the whole process of change begins to happen.

But you need to remember that change is a process that takes time.

What you can grab onto in the midst of this change is that God has not abandoned you. When you feel as if you've been abandoned by family and friends, and you feel an overriding sense of loneliness as you walk through this dark time, know that God has not abandoned you. All the parents I know who have gone through difficult times with their children have learned new ways of understanding God. No wonder—they need new guidance, new information, new resources, and new thoughts about how to get through something they have never experienced, something new and very difficult.

Parents who are at the beginning stages of difficulty with their children are often disgruntled, unhappy, and unsettled as they look for new ways to help their children. If that is you, the challenges you now face demand new answers. And God is now providing you the opportunity to learn something new from Him.

You can also grab onto the fact that God will use this awful situation in your life and your child's life to mold you both in ways you would have never thought possible. I have seen the worst of situations turn into something absolutely amazing. God uses everything and stops at nothing to weave our lives into something beautiful.

Jessica

Jessica's mother and brother, on their way to Alaska, were camping in Canada when a brown bear attacked her mother and began to maul her. Jessica's brother could be heard on videotape telling his mother not to move, to play dead, and the bear would leave. Well, it didn't.

At that moment, a park ranger ran up to the bear to try to distract it, and with one swipe of the bear's paw, the ranger was decapitated. The brother desperately tried to distract the bear, and he himself was injured in the attack. I can hardly imagine what it was like or envision the attack.

Jessica's mother died. Her brother was critically injured. And Jessica had to deal with her mother's absence and the thoughts and visualizations of her death.

I met Jessica when she was 16 and her life was spinning out of control. While she was at Heartlight, she met a fellow she would later marry. Today Jessica and her husband are the proud parents of a little baby.

Did God orchestrate the bear attack so Jessica would one day meet this new fellow, get married, and have a baby that has been a blessing to the whole family? No. But did He use every situation in her life to bring her to the point where she is today? Absolutely.

What Does Hope Feel Like?

If your teen has gradually fallen into a pattern of inappropriate behaviors, he or she will probably take some time to pull out of the dive. As I have stated earlier, a change of the heart is not normally the immediate response to what you have implemented in your home to deal with your teen's behavior. New habits are hard to build into a teen's life. And new rules and policies need some time to take hold. But they will. Just give it some time.

Your teens are going to be teens. But even as teens, they really do want a relationship with you. They would much rather have you as a parent than a friend. God will honor your efforts. Don't give up. Don't give in. But do give your teens all they need at this juncture in their lives. And if you are feeling miserable in the midst of the struggle you're going through, I can guarantee your child feels worse. This is the time they need your presence, your guidance, and your heart.

CHAPTER SIXTEEN

WHERE ARE
THEY NOW?

Using examples of teens I have been with throughout the years would be unfair without telling you how those teens are doing today. I have kept up with each one and want to share with you where they are today. Some are doing well. Some are not. But each is held dear to my heart regardless of their behavior or choices. I've listed each teen in order of their appearance.

Chapter 1

Gracie's parents never quite understood the role they played in their daughter's struggles. As a result, they never changed their strategy to help her. Gracie is doing well. In spite of her parents' struggles, Gracie has blossomed and has gotten on the other side of her rebellion and difficult time.

Michael continued to spiral out of control until age 17, when he finally hit bottom and came to live at Heartlight. He's now married, has three kids, and holds a job as an account executive for a public relations firm in St. Louis, Missouri. He's involved in church and leads a recovery small group for teens. He speaks to teens quite frequently about his time of darkness and has a wonderful relationship with his parents.

Erica recently married a wonderful young man from southern California. Her two kids were flower girls. She's a great mom and a wonderful wife who rarely darkens the door of a church but has a great relationship with her family and a great relationship with the Lord. She has worked through what has happened in her life but hasn't quite worked through who did it.

Brian is in college in northern Virginia and is doing very well. I've always been amazed that an orphan from Russia could learn so much about life through a horse in Texas. Mariah (the horse) has since died, but Brian has come to life. He says he rarely thinks about Russia but would love to relearn the language and do something in the field of international business.

Alan is a dear young man who lives life to its fullest. He's married and has two boys. His wife enjoys keeping up with her three boys. Alan's dad and mom now laugh about their "crazy time" that happened years ago, and they recently told me how proud they are of Alan. After a couple of years in the military, Alan was able to harness his attention deficit disorder and not allow it to control him. He's a salesman who can carry on a conversation with just about anybody. He's a delight to be around, a great dad, and a wonderful husband.

Chapter 3

Adam, my son, divorced his wife and is now feeling the effects of his decisions. His loneliness is an overwhelming thing to watch. Coming to the understanding of how he's wronged people has been a difficult road. He is my son and has taught me how to love someone not just when they do everything right but also when they do things wrong. He can do nothing to make me love him more and nothing to make me love him less.

John and Virginia continued to watch their daughter, Patty, struggle at college. She has shocked them many times throughout her college years. The relationship with Patty is better, but they both say they don't see her much. They do enjoy the peace around their home.

Kyle continues to struggle. And his parents continue to give me updates and catch me up on the situation about every six months. They continue to not listen to me, and Kyle continues to not hear anything they say. I fear that they will lose their son, not because their son is going through a difficult time and making poor choices, but because his parents failed to act and have allowed him to continue on this path that he really doesn't want to be on.

Steve and Tonia finally realized their need to help their son and have been committed to helping him get on the right path. Adam struggled for years with alcohol, and now, after two marriages, three kids, and the death of a child, he's clean and finally getting his life together. He's 40 years old.

Sam and Marty are raising Sarah's child and have learned to adjust their expectations for Sarah. It has made life easier for them. Sarah is a sweet girl who finally married her live-in boyfriend, who has beaten and bruised her through the years. Her drug use has lessened, but not much. She continues to make poor choices, and Sam and Marty continue to fulfill their commitment to love her in ways they never thought possible.

James and Laura learned to quit beating themselves up for not protecting their child and have a great relationship with Tammy, her husband, and her two children. They have finally forgiven the uncle who abused Tammy, who served an eight-year sentence for child molestation (of another child). Tammy went through years of counseling, had difficulty bonding with men most of those years, but has come through her ordeal shining. Rarely does she think about the times that she was molested.

Chapter 4

My dad is an 81-year-old WWII veteran who loves me in ways I really never understood and who probably doesn't understand the ways I have grown to love him. He takes care of my mom, and my mom takes care of him, fulfilling a commitment they made 56 years ago.

Chapter 5

Leigh lives in Kansas City and laughs about the time she spent on the streets. She's married and has three wonderful children, runs a business, and has a wonderful relationship with her parents and family. Oddly, her mother has stated that Leigh's struggles forced their family to work through all their issues, which in turn shaped the depth of relationships they all enjoy today. I'm always excited to hear about what she's doing. She really doesn't care about what people think about her and enjoys a confidence about herself I wish I possessed.

Chapter 6

Ashley is one of the finest kids I've ever met. She has worked through so many difficulties in her life with the help of a mother who loves her dearly and a stepdad who is the hero of all fathers. She tells me she would like to get a degree in counseling—which I have offered to pay for. I would gladly hire her in a heartbeat to work on our staff at Heartlight so she could give her life to others who struggle. Sadly, Ashley's younger sister committed suicide two years ago. Her older sister has been in and out of drug rehab programs. No one can convince me that kids' carrying traumatic experiences just work themselves out, a sentiment I hear much too often.

Kelley has regained her relationship with both her dad and mom and is currently attending college in Tennessee. Her little girl even goes to class with her sometimes. Her dad is very involved in all aspects of her life, and Kelley helps lead a Young Life club in her college town.

Dan should be on stage as a comedian. Instead, he has chosen to be a welder and spends much of his time helping his wife take care of his son. He laughs when he tells me how he's helped his mom and dad work through their problems and has encouraged me to start a Heartlight for parents!

Chapter 7

Brian is married and living in Seattle with his beautiful wife and daughter. He works for his dad's company, is involved in ministry with his church, and can't wait to go to Colorado for a snow skiing vacation.

Chapter 8

Anna and I married 32 years ago. She's my wife, Jan. With a heart of gold and a vision to share the love of God with everyone around her, Jan works at Heartlight, overseeing the counseling program and touching the hearts of others in all she does.

Jamie currently lives in Virginia, going to school and working with preschool kids at her church. She has not allowed the forgotten events of childhood to determine the mood of her life. Whenever I see a young person with a broken arm, I think of her and am strangely warmed by an overwhelming sense of God's protection and grace.

Chapter 9

Angel responded well to her parents and has maintained a great relationship with them both now that she is married. She teaches special education kids with an emphasis in speech therapy. Isn't that amazing? A girl who listened to no one is now teaching kids to communicate. God does have a sense of humor!

Charlie is now in college, living in a college dorm and participating in intramurals. He laughingly calls his high school years his "basement years." He has a wonderful relationship with his parents and is dating an awesome young lady who is an extrovert.

Tracy is now married for a second time. She spends a lot of time with her mother and considers her mom her best friend. She is a delightful young lady with two adorable children.

Chapter 10

Rick and Vicki eventually made the changes in their parenting styles to accommodate the needs of their boys. Their relationships are good, and believe it or not, they all laugh about the devotional times of the early teen years. But the confusion did come with a cost. The opportunities lost during those struggling years aren't easily replaced. They're all trying their best to do so.

Chapter 11

Leslie is currently in college, has brought their family back together, and meets with her parents regularly to discuss ways they can better parent her younger sister, who is in the beginning stages of spinning out of control. She's involved in her church and is thankful for her parents' commitment to her.

Candice calls occasionally as she travels homelessly across the country. The calls are usually for money for a hotel, for a plane ticket, or for some other need. The last time I saw her was two years ago, after a ten-year absence, when she showed up on our doorstep. I got her a room at the local hotel for a night. She's homeless and much the same girl she was 12 years ago when I first met her.

Chapter 12

Anna left home and didn't return. I understand she's living somewhere in Michigan, but none of us really know. Her mother hasn't heard from her in years.

Randy is now over 40 years old and is a wonderful husband, father, and Sunday school teacher. He operates his own business in Tulsa. He and his wife have been married for 22 years, and his mother now lives with them.

Todd, the fellow who always isolated himself, is in college studying to be a computer programmer. Imagine that. His friends tell him that he spends too much time alone, but he's learning to get out more.

Chapter 13

Rebecca calls occasionally to check up on me and to see if her mom has changed any. Her mother calls, asking if we've talked to Rebecca and to "please have her give me a call." Rebecca is a responsible college student who has the maturity of a 30-year-old and loves living life outside of the control of her mom.

Jim is still a very immature and irresponsible young—very young—30-year-old. He acts like a 14-year-old because he's been treated like one his whole life.

Chapter 14

Chris is a professional boxer. Not really! He's a builder in Nashville, Tennessee, and recently got married. Whenever I see someone with a black eye, I think of him and am thankful I no longer transport teens who are spinning out of control.

Phil never connected with me, so I don't have the slightest idea where he is. He's one of the regrets that I carry with me; I feel responsible for the struggles he went through in life. Not because he had them but because I wasn't able to help him because of something I thought was right but was really so wrong. Deceitfulness destroys. Perhaps one day I'll see Phil and will be able to ask for his forgiveness.

Will is a pastor of a Bible church. He would love to tell you about his scar. I was always amazed at this young man's immediate turnaround.

Chapter 15

Bentley still loves Starbucks and has a great relationship with his parents. Bentley will tell you that he's now 30 and can't think of anything wrong with his parents, whom he's grown to love and cherish.

Jessica is married and has a little boy. She is one of the funniest girls I have ever met and would make any father proud. Her testimony to all is how God can take the worst of situations and use it for good.

NOTES

Chapter 1—Hope amid the Conflict

1. "Chavaleh" from the musical FIDDLER ON THE ROOF Words by Sheldon Harnick, Music by Jerry Bock Copyright © 1964 (Renewed) Mayerling Productions Ltd. (Admiinistered by R&H Music) and Jerry Bock Enterprises for the United States and Alley Music Corporation, Trio Music Company, and Jerry Bock Enterprises for the world outside of the United States. Used by permission. All rights reserved.

2. Ursula K. Le Guin, *The Left Hand of Darkness* (New York, NY: Ace Books, 1969, 2000), p. 220.

3. Rick Warren, *The Purpose-Driven Life* (Grand Rapids, Michigan: Zondervan, 2002), p. 17.

Chapter 5—The Problem of Performance-Based Relationships

1. Dan Allender, *How Children Raise Parents* (Colorado Springs: WaterBrook Press, 2003), p. 89.

Chapter 6—Why Does My Child Act This Way?

1. J.R.R. Tolkien, *The Fellowship of the Ring* (New York: Houghton Mifflin, 2004), p. 348.

2. John Armor, " 'I Did It...Because I Could'—Bill Clinton Writes His Own Epitaph," *Free Republic,* June 26, 2004.

Chapter 7—The Importance of Pain

1. C.S. Lewis, *The Problem of Pain* (New York: HarperCollins, 2001), p. 91.

Chapter 8—Loss

1. David Damico, *The Faces of Rage* (Colorado Springs: NavPress, 1992), p. 47.

Chapter 11—Setting Boundaries

1. Henry Cloud and John Townsend, *Boundaries* (Grand Rapids: Zondervan, 1992), p. 29.

Chapter 12—Allowing Your Child to Be in Control

1. Mark Twain, *A Tramp Abroad* (Whitefish, MT: Kessinger Publishing, 2004), p. 301.

2. Henry Cloud and John Townsend, *Boundaries* (Grand Rapids: Zondervan, 1992), p. 78.

Chapter 13—Building Maturity by Giving Responsibility

1. David Damico, *The Faces of* Rage (Colorado Springs: NavPress, 1992), p. 65.

2. Oscar Wilde, *Lady Windermere's Fan* (Mineola, NY: Dover Publications, 1998), p. 50.

3. James A. Belasco and Ralph C. Stayer, *Flight of the Buffalo* (New York: Warner Books, 1993), p. 312.

4. Andy Law, *Creative Company* (New York: John Wiley & Sons, Inc., 1999), p. 86.

About the Author

Mark and Jan Gregston began their work with teens 30 years ago, when Mark was a youth minister at First Methodist Church in Tulsa, Oklahoma. Their involvement with Young Life moved them to open their home to work with those who were struggling through crisis family problems. During the 1980s, while living at Kanakuk Kamp in Branson, Missouri, Mark was the area director for Young Life and a part of the leadership team for Doulos Ministries, where he helped start a residential program. In 1989, Mark and Jan moved with their two children, Adam and Melissa, to Hallsville, Texas. Here they started Heartlight Ministries, dedicated to providing an effective program for struggling and troubled teens in family crisis.

Believing that an atmosphere of relationships creates an arena for change, Mark and Jan share their lives through retreats, speaking engagements, counseling, hosting a national radio program for parents, and directing the Heartlight Ministries residential program. Mark travels most weekends speaking or leading Dealing with Today's Teens seminars in cities across the nation.

For more information, visit www.HeartlightMinistries.org.